CAPITAL PUNISHMENT

CAPITAL PUNISHMENT

Capital Punishment

How a private equity firm's lies
left me broke and ruined my life

by Sharon Wright

CAPITAL PUNISHMENT

Capital Punishment
Copyright © 2025 Sharon Wright Productions 1 Ltd
(ALL RIGHTS RESERVED)

ISBN:9798283365022

DISCLAIMER

This is a true story of my lived experience. For legal reasons most of the names and details have been changed to protect privacy. I've done my best to be faithful to my experiences, and when possible, have consulted others who were also present during that time. I relied on letters, journals, interviews, and conversations I had with many people who appear in these pages, as well as my own memory. In some cases, I have edited conversations for brevity. To protect the anonymity of certain individuals and businesses herein mentioned, I have modified or entirely changed their names.

COPYRIGHT

All rights reserved. No portion of this book may be reproduced in any form without written permission from the publisher or author, except as permitted by U.S. copyright law. This publication is designed to provide accurate and authoritative information in regard to the subject matter covered.

ALL RIGHTS RESERVED

This book or parts thereof may not be reproduced in any form, stored in any retrieval system, or transmitted in any form by any means, electronic, mechanical, photocopy, recording, or otherwise, without prior written permission of the publisher, except as provided by United States of America copyright law.

For permission requests contact: sharon@sharonwright.com

CAPITAL PUNISHMENT

*"For our struggle is not against flesh and blood,
but against the rulers, against the authorities,
against the powers of this dark world and against
the spiritual forces of evil in the heavenly realms."*

Ephesians 6:12

CAPITAL PUNISHMENT

CHAPTER 1

The Nightmare Before Christmas

I woke up after less than an hour of tortured "sleep" feeling nauseous despite having barely eaten for over a week. My whole body ached for rest. I vaguely hoped I was in some kind of Matrix-style nightmare. But no. It was all real.

It was 22nd of December 2023, the day after our High Court judgement in London. It had been six days since we'd received notice that we'd been accused of theft and fraud. I'd been too ill to attend the proceedings, so my husband John had gone on his own taking a doctor's note to inform the judge I had pneumonia. Now he'd returned to our home in Lincolnshire.

As well as feeling sick with disgust at the judge's decision I was struck with panic. Christmas was just a couple of days away but as usual I'd left everything until the last minute. Amazingly, I always managed to deliver – or should I say Amazon Prime did.

I'd tried to pick out some gifts but my thoughts were going in all different directions. As I clicked through the pages I couldn't focus and had no idea what to buy. It was the last day to get presents for the grandchildren but I couldn't move. I just laid on my bed in the dark with the curtains closed.

John came in to remind me we had a Zoom call with the lawyers to go over the High Court hearing and said he'd choose the kids' presents. Even if he didn't put much thought into it, anything was better than nothing. The grandchildren would be so disappointed if they thought we'd forgotten them.

I forced myself to get out of bed. As I went downstairs, I felt repelled by everything around me. I hated this house. It should have been our dream forever home, but to me it was just a monument to heartache and disaster. Design problems had meant extra costs and endless delays. We were in a legal stalemate with the architect and the work still wasn't finished.

I sat at the kitchen island and looked at John. He was trying his best to stay strong but I could see he felt hopeless like me. He was probably even more beaten down, having endured a lifetime of broken promises, a massive financial betrayal by a former business partner and now this.

I will admit at this point he wasn't my favourite person. If only he'd been more forceful when it came to dealing with the American investment firm that had originally lent him most of the money to buy Buildadeck Fencing and Decking UK in 2016 he could have made sure we had more protection against them.

My alarm bells had been ringing since John had agreed with the Americans to buy my decking installation company Buildadeck East Coast. My thriving business had now been incorporated into Buildadeck Fencing and Decking UK, but I still hadn't been fully paid for it. Whenever I haven't listened to my gut things have always backfired. This time was no different.

The Zoom call with our counsel was the last straw. Having paid them tens of thousands already all I heard was the next round of litigation would cost us another £65,000. I was consumed by rage due to their failure to properly present the case for our defence.

CAPITAL PUNISHMENT

All the evidence showed Commercide Ventures had manufactured a case against John and I and were falsely accusing us of theft and fraud. They were also accusing John of failing in his fiduciary duties by making payments that were not in Commercide's best interests but in his own.

Under the instruction of Commercide, Buildadeck's barrister had asked for a freezing order on John's assets plus an injunction on my house and had outlined their claims to a judge in our absence on Friday December 15th 2023. When only one side presents their case, this is known as an ex-parté request.

We were only notified of their actions the following day when John found two hand delivered envelopes stuck to the door. Nobody works on the weekend, so this gave us just three days to find a lawyer, assemble our evidence and brief our legal team before the hearing on 21st December 2023.

It was ridiculously short notice and technically a breach of process. In addition, I'd been too ill to attend and properly explain why their claims were groundless. Why hadn't our barrister got the hearing adjourned until after the New Year to give us time to prepare? That was their first huge mistake. Incredibly, they went on to make even worse ones than that!

Speaking your mind when you are furious is never a good idea, even if your grievances are justified. This would be a lesson that I would learn over the course of the following year. John remained calm because he knew we still needed legal representation.

John and I have both suffered major traumas in our lives. John felt he'd been cheated out of £36 million after his business partner refused to honour their agreement and pay him for his share of Safestyle. Due to having to pay massive court costs he was made bankrupt. Most people would never recover from that kind of loss, but I watched him literally get back on his feet after a life-threatening illness where the doctors said he'd never walk again.

Now the same thing was all happening again, but this time I was involved. We'd lost Buildadeck – or should I say had it taken from us – after running it together for several years. We had taken it to a profitable, expanding business employing around 200 workers to become the UK's premier fencing and decking company.

The judge had granted their request for a freezing order and all of the money from the sale of my house would now be held by the court, plus I couldn't sell it without the court's permission. The judge also ruled that my house couldn't be used as collateral to pay for our legal defence. How were we supposed to defend ourselves going forward? It was as if we'd already been given a "guilty" verdict, although the judge went to great lengths to point out he made no such finding.

I couldn't comprehend how Nick Smith, the CEO of Commercide Ventures could be this evil. How could anyone even come up with such a malicious, premeditated plan? It was lawfare of the most ruthless, malicious kind. They'd weaponised the legal system against us, then timed their assault to ensure we'd suffer the maximum distress over Christmas and struggle to find legal representation.

I left John to handle the rest of the call and went back upstairs. My blood pressure was sky high and my head was spinning. The fear, frustration and rage had surged out of me like lava from an active volcano. I'd let our legal team know exactly what I thought of them. I was furious at how poorly they had handled our case and overlooked vital evidence.

The crux of the issue was that in 2021 I had bought some land for £30,000 and used Buildadeck's solicitor to handle the transaction. I'd trusted John to reimburse the money to the company's bank account, but to my dismay he hadn't paid back the full amount.

Their second claim was that I'd fraudulently used company funds to buy materials to build my new house. All the directors knew I'd been offsetting them against the money I was still owed for the sale of my installation business to Buildadeck.

Nick had told me that he was fine with the payment of the money that was owed to me, but of course didn't put anything in writing. Now he was denying he'd ever given authorisation.

We had given our lawyers all the evidence they needed to show that every building material purchase I'd made had been accurately deducted from what I was owed for the sale of my installation businesses. There was also evidence to show that John had deposited all but £5,000 of the money I'd used to pay for the land on the day and there was evidence he had deposited £50,000 the previous month. But in both instances our legal team had failed to submit the vital bank statements to the judge!

Without the benefit of these documents the judge said Buildadeck's claims would have to be resolved at trial. In his view they had a "good arguable case" that John may have authorised payments that "weren't in the company's interests" and that "assets may have been moved or concealed" without proper authorisation. He even said he was surprised we had failed to provide the necessary materials that could have cleared up the matter.

The freezing order meant John's bank accounts were inaccessible to us and we were only allowed a limited sum for living expenses and legal fees. The order made by the judge did grant me permission to continue trying to sell my house, but it said I had to return to court before any contract could be signed. In addition, it said I was not allowed to use the property as security to raise funds to cover our legal fees.

I vented my frustration at our lawyers and told them they had badly let us down. Why didn't they present the evidence that clearly showed no money had been stolen? Neither John or I had breached our fiduciary duties either. In fact, we'd expanded the business and Buildadeck was making good profits even through and beyond the Covid pandemic.

Covid was when Commercide saw an opportunity to poach the company, get John and myself off Buildadeck's list of creditors and concoct an excuse to get their hands on my house. To have any "dirt" on me they had to create a link between my property and Buildadeck.

They couldn't get a freezing order against me any other way because I wasn't a risk. I had had no history of avoiding debt, no county court judgements and a clean credit history. So, they claimed I dishonestly used company funds to buy land and building materials.

I believe they hatched this plan thinking I wouldn't be able to handle the litigation and would just go quietly rather than face them in court. Well, that's my theory and considering all the factors involved, it looks pretty sound.

Nick and his henchmen must be laughing! Our hugely expensive lawyers may as well have been working for them for all the good they'd done us.

Now everyone thought I was a thief. I couldn't sell my house without the court's permission and we couldn't afford further legal representation. My reputation was in ruins and everything I'd worked for all my life was about to be taken from me under false pretences.

The injustice was too much to bear.

CAPITAL PUNISHMENT

CHAPTER 2

I'm Sent Over the Edge

I sat on the bed and reached across to open my bedside cabinet. Paracetamol and aspirin were all I could find. I pressed all the tablets out of their foil packets and held them in my hand. My heart was beating so fast. I actually wished it would beat faster and explode. At least if I had a heart attack, I wouldn't be committing a sin against God by killing myself.

I'd been here before but had never planned it out properly. Now I had all the pills in my hand I felt like I was on the edge of a cliff and one tiny push would send me falling into my grave. Surely my family and friends would forgive me as they knew about all the traumas I'd been through over the years. How many times had they told me they wouldn't have been able to cope?

Then my mind fell into the most painful part of this whole thing: the mind-blowing level of betrayal by Paul, my long-time friend and business partner who'd helped build our decking installation business.

He knew how much John and I had been through with his Safestyle situation and my "Dragons' Den" nightmare. For anyone who is unfamiliar with what happened I will briefly describe my ordeal.

In 2008 I delivered one of the most successful pitches in the history of this TV series. In this show inventors pitch their ideas to a panel of judges, a.k.a., "dragons" in the hope they will invest in their business. Two of the judges were James Caan and Duncan Bannatyne.

They were impressed by my presentation and offered me £80,000 for a share of my business which was to manufacture and supply a unique magnetic tool to pull cables through cavity walls. However, their offer turned out to be a loan of £22,600 which was packaged in such a way it gave them control of my company. I had to take legal action to terminate the contract.

In June 2017 Paul and I had set up a decking installation company and were working alongside John and his new business Buildadeck Fencing and Decking he'd acquired the previous year.

Paul knew how much John and I had both suffered. He'd witnessed our raw emotions because we trusted him like family and shared everything with him. But when he had to choose a side, he chose Commercide because they were more powerful than us. He didn't defend us or tell the truth. He put himself first and threw all our years of mutual loyalty and respect in the gutter.

I thought of my daughter Molly and her two little girls. Thankfully, I'd enjoyed spending lots of time with them and it had been pure pleasure watching them grow into beautiful humans. Their innocence and love for me was what I had been missing my whole life. It was so unconditional. They loved me to their full capacity without any judgement. All they wanted was my time and I had that in abundance since I'd stopped working at Buildadeck Fencing and Decking UK in October 2020. I'll explain more about that painful chapter later.

I sobbed, angry that I was going to be robbed of any more precious moments with them. They would never really know me because they were so young. My only comfort was that I could watch and guide them from the above.

People say I'm strong because I've been through so much in my 55 years of life, which friends describe as an intense version of Eastenders. I've had no choice but to stand tall and just keep going. I had employees to look after and a family to support. But at this moment I couldn't do it anymore. Life was too cruel. I was desperate to exit the world.

As I stared into space while the devil on my shoulder screamed at me, "Just do it! Go on, kill yourself and get it over with…"

Then I heard footsteps coming up the stairs. John had finished talking to the lawyers. He tried to put my mind at ease by telling me Nick wouldn't get away with stealing our shares in Buildadeck, or the company or my home. But his words triggered that extra bit of emotion that I just couldn't handle.

Seeing the pills in my hand he instinctively grabbed my wrists and held them tight, but my determination was stronger than his grip. Nothing was going to stop me putting an end to this hell. I threw the tablets into my throat and reached for some water to swallow them down.

I will never forget John's look of horror and desperation. He didn't know what to do. He stared at all the empty packets of pills on the bed. Terror and disbelief spread across his face. All I felt was relief. It was done. There was no going back. I was on my way to peace…

For anyone reading this who has witnessed or known someone end their life, you have to understand that they are not selfish. If an act of suicide is not a spontaneous response to a traumatic event, that person will have considered their options long and hard and will have lived with their thoughts and their pain for a long time.

It's not one situation that tips them over the edge. It's a whole accumulation of events and realisations that leaves them so overwhelmed they can't see a future that isn't one of suffering. All they want is to be free from the torture in their head.

Because they have withdrawn from the world they can't rationalise their thoughts. Anyone who cuts themself off like this needs the right support and help. Sometimes all it takes is for their fear and pain to be acknowledged.

John panicked and ran downstairs to grab his phone to call 999. I laid down on the bed and sent my last text messages to Paul and Nick. As you can tell by the tone of my words, I really did not care what I said or how I said it. I was ready to die.

My message to Nick read, "I have taken an overdose. You will see Paul was aware of everything and Gary because you gave us permission. I suffer from mental health. I wanted you to be the last person I message after I tried to reach out to you. Goodbye."

Paul's was, "I have taken an overdose. Your own self was more important. You have lied to Nick and the proof will come out. Goodbye fucking world."

Then I called my daughter Molly and my brothers to tell them what I'd had done. I apologised and explained the reasons for my decision and told them I needed nothing from them.

Molly's voice was shaking as she spoke. Being a nurse, she tried her best to stay calm and ask rational questions about what I had taken and where John was to keep me on the phone. She switched into carer mode and spoke to me with empathy and concern.

When I told one of my brothers what I'd done he screamed, "I can't believe how you could do such a thing!" His anger was the reaction I'd expected but I knew he'd eventually forgive me. My other brother was sympathetic and said he was getting in his car and coming over immediately.

I couldn't call my dad. I didn't want to hear the anguish in his voice. My mum had died just a few years earlier and I'd seen him grieve every day from the loss. He was going through the motions of living until the day he could be reunited with her again.

After being rushed to hospital the first thing they did was my bloodwork to see how much damage had been done to my liver. There was no point pumping my stomach because the pills were already in my system. Hospitals had stopped doing this anyway because it was pointless in most cases.

I wanted to be on my own and told John to leave. I couldn't cope with seeing the grief and disbelief on his face. He sat in the waiting room in A & E in case I needed him at some point. All I wanted was to be left alone to sit in the space in my head. I didn't even want to talk to the medical staff. There was no more crying or screaming. I felt at peace. There was no going back.

Four hours later I realised I didn't want to stop living. I didn't want to die!

I wanted to stay alive! Apparently, many people who attempt suicide regret it as soon as they act upon their decision. I ended up being one of them. Now I was just numb, sitting on a chair behind a curtain hidden from view, contemplating the mess that was my life.

CAPITAL PUNISHMENT

The doctors and nurses came in to check my vitals every half hour while I waited to find out if I'd irreversibly harmed my liver and would suffer a slow and painful death.

My phone buzzed constantly with calls from my loved ones, but I couldn't speak to any of them. I was too ashamed of what I'd done. I just wanted to wallow quietly in self-pity because it was a familiar place. At least doing that I knew wasn't affecting anyone.

To my huge relief, a doctor told me the paracetamol and Anadin Extra I'd swallowed had become quite dilute and no lasting damage had been done. I wasn't going to die slowly in agony and my liver was fine.

Someone from the hospital's crisis team would be with me shortly to assess my mental state and decide how I could best be helped going forward. All I wanted was to go home and sleep into oblivion.

I'd had therapy many times over the years and was exhausted with having to explain everything repeatedly. Nobody could help me so what was the point? My life was bullshit dotted with a few pleasurable experiences which were always short lived before the next injustice or disappointment came out of nowhere.

I briefly reflected on all the shit I'd endured starting from the age of five. I've never spoken much about some events because I was scared of upsetting people's feelings. But now that last bit of fear in me had gone. Everything had to be brought out into the open because I couldn't carry the burden of past sufferings on top of what I was already dealing with.

The counsellor took me into a cold hospital room and asked what had happened that brought me to A & E that day. How the fucking hell was I supposed to answer that question? Everything had been so horrendous with all the lies and accusations against us. It was so terrible you couldn't write it down (well technically you can, because that's what I've attempted to do here).

Throughout my life any counselling has been stored in my memory under "trauma" and this latest episode would be shut away with all the rest. But to my surprise, the counsellor made me feel unjudged and was genuinely interested in why I felt so strongly that I had to end my life.

Over the next two hours I poured everything out – literally – while she listened with a look of sympathy as the snot and tears ran uncontrollably from my face. I told her I hated my life and myself for the pain I had put my loved ones through. Nothing I had done had ever been worth it and I had failed as a mother and a human being. Yet all I had ever done was try my very best, work hard and give what I could to others.

The money, the nice cars and the big house was all a façade. It all presented an image of success which people assumed meant happiness. But in reality, I felt unheard, hopeless and tormented by the fact that contentment was so elusive to me. I would often think it would be better if I wasn't here so I wouldn't hinder or upset others anymore.

After explaining all the battles I'd fought throughout my life: my bulimia, the terrible betrayals in my personal and business life and all the legal issues with Commercide, the counsellor agreed that it was "a lot."

She loaded me up with antidepressants and sleeping tablets and told me what my choices were. I could either be referred to a psychiatric hospital or receive out-patient follow up care. I told her I was safe to return home. All I wanted to do was sleep.

As we left the hospital John told me that while he'd been waiting for the ambulance to arrive, Paul had called to ask if he was with me because of the message I'd sent him. Hearing this I thought I could possibly forgive him for siding with the enemy, because at least he'd shown an ounce of compassion. But his treachery still filled me with disbelief.

As for Nick Smith, the founder of Commercide Ventures, there was nothing. Not a call to ask if I was okay. Not even a text message in response to mine informing I was about to take my own life. He had zero concern for me. Why was I surprised?

I guess that's the standard response of the corporate psychopath: no empathy, accountability or remorse. These money-hungry wolves in sheep's clothing are eloquent and charming at first so they can trick people into thinking they're benevolent and supportive before going in for the kill. Money, power and control are all they care about.

I know of people who have committed suicide or been reduced to human wreckage after falling a victim to this type of predator. Others have lost everything and have ended up settling out of court for a pittance because they couldn't handle the stress of the legal process.

Private equity capital investment companies work closely with law firms who are just as important a part of their business as their accountants, making them a formidable opponent. Essentially, what they do is raise a large fund (usually from affluent investors) and reinvest these funds to reap the biggest possible profits.

Coercion, manipulation and corruption in business is well known, but those on the receiving end don't fight long and hard enough for their voices to be heard. The trusting and the honest are destroyed financially, physically and emotionally. If they are lucky, they might escape with their sanity and a roof over their heads after years spent toiling to grow their companies.

Only a few like me will fight to defend their good name no matter the cost to their mental health, their personal life or their finances. I have been wrongly accused of theft and fraud by a company who has committed those very same crimes against me. But I refuse to be a victim in this and will do everything I can to change the system so no one else falls prey to these private equity companies whose goal is profit at any cost; human lives included.

I now wonder whether this has been my mission all along, to learn the most painful lessons and be part of the opposition to change things for the better.

What you are about to read is a true, accurate and detailed account of the events of the past two years. As John and I face the fight of our lives this tell-all book will be our legacy as well as our voice should anything "happen" to us before justice is served.

CAPITAL PUNISHMENT

CHAPTER 3

Bizarre Things Start to Happen

Shortly after John and I were fired from Buildadeck Fencing and Decking UK in April 2023 we put our almost fully built new house on the market, but so far there had been very little response. I used to be an estate agent and I know higher priced houses take time to sell. Ours had cost just over £2.2 million to build. If we were in London, it would have sold faster, but Lincolnshire was a different story as millionaires are thinner on the ground.

One of our first viewings was for a professor at Cambridge University. He was randomly lingering at the end of our drive so we invited him in to take a look around. As we were chatting, he mentioned that he'd helped to develop the Moderna vaccine from Covid days. He was impressed by the house, but later decided it was too expensive.

Then there was a young couple called Charlene and Ant who arrived with their small child. They'd unfortunately suffered at the hands of the NHS who'd been negligent in their baby's delivery, leaving him with a severe, long-term disability. Now they were in the process of claiming compensation.

They also loved the house and said it ticked every box. They wanted to know if we would accept £2.2 million. (Coincidentally, this was the exact same amount Commercide originally agreed to pay me for my installation businesses.)

It was a sum that would give us the freedom to move on with our lives, buy a smaller house with no mortgage and leave us with money to fund another business, so we accepted their offer. Unfortunately, the compensation process is extremely long and the buyers withdrew, which was a blow because financially things were getting tight.

Looking back, I realised that I'd never really been careful with my money because I was always confident I would generate more. Over the years I must have casually spent tens of thousands without a second thought.

I had helped my daughter buy her first house and car and gifted my best friend's daughter a new Prius when she passed her test. I'd taken friends on luxury holidays and mostly paid for my daughter's lavish wedding. I've always taken pleasure in spending money on others. But now our bank balance was low and thoughts of regret started entering my mind. Things would have been so different if I'd invested all my spare money and kept it for myself.

On December 9th 2023, (six days before Buildadeck's barrister went to court to request a freezing order to stop me from selling my house) my estate agent called to say cash buyers – a young man and woman in their mid-20s with a two-year old – were interested in seeing the property. They all arrived in a taxi the next day, which I thought was strange.

The young woman, whose name was Elina, explained that her car was in the garage. I knew by looking at their shoes, the child's buggy and the way they were dressed that there was no way they could afford the house. They stayed for two and a half hours looking around the property and asking questions, but I had mentally switched off after an hour.

Then they ordered a taxi to come and collect them. It got a bit awkward while they were waiting as we had exhausted just about every subject of conversation. Elina asked if she could take another look around on her own. By now I was sure they were time-wasters and I couldn't hide my frustration.

I asked how she could afford a £2.5 million house at the age of 26 and pay with cash. She replied that her mother was a Lithuanian Euro lottery winner and she wanted to relocate to the area. It was a strange answer, but I gave her the benefit of the doubt and said nothing more.

A few days later Elina's estate agent called to say her clients would give us the full £2.5 million asking price. I was shocked! John said I should never judge a book by its cover. Maybe he was right.

The same day, Elina sent the proof of funds to our estate agent and to her solicitor. There were two statements from reputable banks. One showed a balance of just over £2.5 million and the other of over £4.6 million.

Elina informed our estate agent that they wanted to move fast and needed to be in the house before her second baby arrived next year in March. John and I celebrated with a Chinese takeaway. A quick sale at full asking price with no chain was almost too good to be true!

I added Elina to my list of Facebook friends so I could find out more about her. From studying her old posts, it appeared that she lived in a small rented house. If she had so much money in the bank, why was she renting? Maybe she didn't want to buy something unless it was the perfect forever home and was waiting. I was so focused on the sale taking place that I talked myself out of my suspicions.

Elina and I texted each other daily. She told me her mother wanted to see the house, so we agreed on a date for a second viewing. But on the day she was supposed to visit, Elina told us she'd missed her flight and would now be arriving the following day. Then she explained that because she was only staying a few days and had limited time, the viewing had to be cancelled. What? Surely looking at the house should have been her main priority?

Both sets of solicitors knew everyone wanted to exchange contracts before Christmas and complete the sale in the New Year. We were even paying extra fees to push the process through faster. Elina wanted me to take the property off the market, but I told her we would only do this after she had signed the paperwork and she had committed to buy it.

When this didn't happen, Elina proceeded to send multiple daily updates to reassure us that they were still interested and moving ahead. But every time she planned to do something to complete the process, she'd send me another message saying there'd been another hitch. One day I counted 22 texts alone!

Elina finally told us a deposit had been sent via her private bank manager who had expedited the payment. Of course there was a problem. Apparently, she had changed solicitors which meant everything was held up.

Even when our estate agent pointed out to us that nothing was happening on the buyer's side, I still believed Elina's explanations. Surely nobody would spend so much of their time convincing someone of a made-up situation? It made no sense.

Here are some examples of her messages:

Elina: "Hi Sharon, I've just now seen the email from the solicitor regarding deposit. He will have it by the morning as I won't be able to make it to the branch as it closes in 20 mins but I will get to them by 9.30 am. He said the rest of the paperwork he needs by Friday, but sending that over now xx.

Me: "OK keep me posted xx

Elina: "I will do. I would of done it today, but my mobile app won't let me do more than £10k a day in transfers, so I need the branch to do a larger sum. Might need it changing somehow, but I will ask tomorrow xx"

Me: "I am the same. I can do £20k a day but if u go into the bank they will be able to do it there and then same as mine xx"

Elina: "Yep they will be able to do it without an issue xx"

Me: "Have you now sent the post office documents? I have had my solicitors preparing the contracts but she said they still haven't been sent - r u doing that today? xx

Elina: "Yes we are very excited."

Me: "Have you spoken with your solicitors?"

Elina: "Just tried ringing and no answer. Will try again after the bank."

Then she sent me a voicemail saying the money had been sent. Of course it hadn't been. This kind of back and forth continued every single day for over a month.

The estate agent kept raising her concerns and contacted Elina's solicitors to see if she had been in to see them. They said she had taken copies of documents, but not originals as they requested. Yet another excuse for a delay.

I have to admit now that I am embarrassed that I fell for all this bullshit. I wanted to believe Elina's excuses because I was so desperate for the sale to happen. Then all the pressure we were under would then be lifted.

In January 2024 it was obvious to us that Elina was stringing us along and I began to suspect that Nick or someone else at Commercide must have hired her to act as a potential buyer to raise our hopes. Remember, she turned up around two weeks before the freezing order to stop me selling my house was granted. It would have an even more devastating effect if we thought we had a cash buyer lined up willing to pay the full asking price.

When you hear about all the other strange "visitors" and "friends" who turned up in my life later you may also agree that perhaps some coordinated strategy was in play. I will leave it up to you to draw your own conclusions.

CHAPTER 4

Buildadeck's False Accusations

Six days before our High Court hearing on 21st December 2023, I'd driven over to see my best friend Christine with gifts for her and her daughter. John was at home doing some work. When he called, I knew something was wrong. He told me to come home as soon as possible because we had a serious problem.

Every situation was running through my mind. What could be so important that he had to tell me in person. I worried it was another serious health issue as he'd been through so many in the past.

In 2008 he had an operation to remove a benign tumour from his pelvis. The surgeon accidentally cut through his femoral artery. He lost 16 pints of blood and died on the operating table twice. After this he needed more surgeries to save his life due to problems with his arteries. During 2022 and 2023 he'd had three near-death experiences alone due to infections following more surgeries.

Every few months something major would happen and I'd end up in tears worrying that this was it. I had to make many distressing phone calls to his sons, which in themselves had taken a toll. They say a cat has nine lives. John has had at least 20 at the last count!

As I pulled up the drive I saw John waiting for me at the front door. He was shaking. "Tell me what's happened," I said, at my wits end with worry. He produced a thick brown envelope addressed to me and said we had both been served papers from the court.

CAPITAL PUNISHMENT

Each of our packages contained the same 300 pages listing all the charges against us. The documents had been delivered in person by a courier. We also received a letter from the High Court in London telling us to attend a hearing on the 21st of December, just days before Christmas.

At this point I was shaking too. I didn't understand what was happening or what we'd done. Panic seized my whole body. I'd never done anything wrong in my life. I had never even had any dealings with the police, never mind received a court summons.

John explained that Buildadeck on the instructions of Commercide Ventures was accusing us of fraud, misappropriation of funds and breach of our fiduciary duties. What the hell?

I asked him what that meant. None of it made sense. He sat me down and said Buildadeck's new directors had been to court to apply to put a freezing order on my house to prevent me from selling it. They had also applied to have John's bank account frozen.

I zoned out from fear. I watched John's lips move as I saw him speak but was unable to process any of the words. Sheer shock stopped my brain from processing anything much at all. I must have smoked five cigarettes in the space of ten minutes. It took me about two hours to properly hear what John was saying.

A whole raft of false accusations had been drawn up by Commercide's legal team in an effort to destroy our reputations and leave us both personally and financially ruined. Despite still being owed hundreds of thousands for the sale of my business, Commercide had the gall to accuse me of stealing from my own company! I couldn't believe anyone would be capable of manufacturing such a dishonest and underhand scheme.

John told me he'd read through all of their allegations and they were all fabricated with no supporting evidence, but unfortunately, we had no choice but to defend ourselves which would be a very costly and lengthy process. These predators could slow things down to a snail's pace if it suited them. Omg! It would take years to expose their scam!

In a moment of realisation my life flashed before me. I'd put almost every spare penny I had into building this house. I'd paid for it so therefore it was all in my name. Before that, we lived in a beautiful converted barn in York which stood in two acres of land. However, the access to it was through a piece of our neighbour's farmland which he never used or maintained. I was keeping horses at the time, so I agreed to buy it for £30,000.

I was keen to pay the farmer because I was afraid that he'd change his mind. As I didn't have a solicitor, to save time I asked if I could ask the one John used at Buildadeck to oversee the deal. The solicitor knew me and was a friend of John's so it made sense. Plus, I knew he'd get things done quickly.

My bank account only allowed me to transfer £20,000 a day. As I struggled to set up new payees using the card reader because of my ADHD I usually asked my daughter or John, who were already established payees, to forward the money on to the recipient for me. I have done this for as long as I can remember.

A further complication was because the solicitors had never acted for me before, they were unable to accept money directly from me without carrying out the requisite checks. I asked John for advice and he said it could be paid through Buildadeck.

I paid two lots of £15,000 to John which he then transferred into Buildadeck's bank account, or that's what I was led to believe. Later on, I discovered only £25,000 was paid in and not the full £30,000. As he had £50,000 in his director's loan account, he instructed Buildadeck's account team to deduct the remaining £5000 from that account.

A few days later, I transferred a further £2,200 for legal fees. It was all fully traceable and Buildadeck's finance director was aware of the transactions as well as the two other company directors. Yet Buildadeck was now claiming that I had bought the land using their money so the land belonged to the company and not me. Their documents also alleged that since it had been sold and the funds used to buy and build my house in Scunthorpe, my new property partially belonged to them too.

In addition, the directors at Buildadeck – under the instruction of Commercide – had listed around £152,000 of materials that had been purchased through the company, supposedly without their prior permission, thereby entitling them to an even bigger share of my new house.

They know I'd never steal anything! It's against all my principles and more importantly, guilt is a burden I could never carry. I despise liars, cheats and thieves. Exploiting others goes against everything I stand for. How dare they accuse me of theft!

All the directors were aware that I'd been offsetting some personal expenses against my deferred consideration (the money Buildadeck still owed me) for my installation business. Everyone had been fine with the arrangement. I was mindful to make sure these records were meticulously kept to avoid the slightest discrepancy.

Another of their sham accusations was that John had used his company credit card fraudulently and had racked up nearly £192,000 in private expenses over the four years from 2019 to 2022. In fact, the true figure was around £44,000.

John occasionally used the card for private expenses which were offset against the balance in his loan account. During that four-year period, his private expenditure totalled £44,069. Everything was done with complete transparency. In addition to this, all of Buildadeck's accounts were audited and received a clean report every year.

In late July 2023, around three months after he was fired, one of the directors contacted him to say that Commercide were unhappy because Buildadeck was being chased for an outstanding amount of £18,231.24 on his company credit card. John knew some of this balance would have been personal which is why he had given a personal guarantee to the credit card company that he would pay off any debt if the business couldn't.

John agreed with Paul that he would pay 25% of the balance and Buildadeck would pay the rest. This was confirmed in a text message from John on 11th August 2023. On 14th August he paid £4,550 towards the balance and sent a screenshot of the transaction to Paul. We both believed this was the end of the matter.

On 27th September 2023 John received a letter from Buildadeck's solicitors asking him to clarify payments totalling around £400,000, which included the £192,000 on his company credit card. John responded, "Send me the Deferred Consideration and Director's loan accounts and I will provide a full, substantive response."

Buildadeck refused. This went back and forth over a few more emails. Then they went silent. We didn't hear another word from them until we were personally served on 16th December 2023.

All Commercide's groundless claims were designed to smear our characters and were an important part of their cynical strategy. They were trying to destroy us using psychological warfare at an extreme level you only see in films.

They probably anticipated that John and I would be so shocked at having to deal with such a blatant barrage of lies we'd surrender to their will, crumble when it got to court or take ourselves out.

Something told me they'd done this before.

CHAPTER 5

A Shocking Judgement

The freezing order on the sale of our house meant I couldn't sell it without permission from the court and even if it was granted, all the money from the sale would be held by the court pending the outcome of the trial which was months, if not years away.

As an additional twist of the knife, Buildadeck's claims against us were signed by my ex-business partner and once long-time friend, Paul.

After we received those hand delivered envelopes full of false accusations, John immediately called Paul to ask him what the hell was happening. He explained to John that Commercide had paid a firm of solicitors to assemble a list of complaints against us on Buildadeck's behalf, but every time they amended the documents, he had refused to sign them because none of the contents were true.

Paul also said he told Nick that he would not go to court and lie on the stand to which Nick replied that would never get that far because John and I would be desperate to settle and that we'd rather pay something and walk away than engage in a long, expensive legal battle.

We called several solicitors, but nobody was answering their phones. It was the weekend before Christmas and most practices had closed, so we started collecting all the materials for our defence that we could find at home. Very wisely, John had emailed himself copies of a lot of relevant documents as "security" in the event that something like this happened.

We didn't sleep or eat and worked through the days and nights until the morning of Monday 18th December which was three days before the hearing.

I was a mess. I was constantly crying and screaming in frustration and disbelief. I felt so ashamed that I could be accused of doing something so underhanded. I knew people would associate me with this crime not knowing the facts of the matter. It was defamation of character and the weaponisation of the legal system. It was pure evil!

If I had suffered this kind of abuse in a relationship it would be considered a criminal offence. But in the commercial world companies can inflict huge personal pain and suffering – even driving victims to commit suicide – with impunity. Because psychological and financial abuse is invisible, many victims say it's worse than physical abuse.

John, as always, remained logical and kept working, stoically gathering up as much evidence as he could. But it was all rushed. We needed information that was on the servers at work which we thought we no longer had access to. These predators had created their own perfect storm.

After many hours on the phone, we finally found a solicitor in Scotland who my friend Rita had recommended. Apparently, she went to school with her. (I later discovered Rita was not the ally I thought she was, given everything that transpired as well as the group of people she associated with.)

On the day before the hearing in London, John had to rush me to the doctor because I was sure I was having a heart attack. I couldn't breathe because of the pain in my chest. I hadn't slept for even a minute for six days and had lost a stone in weight.

All I'd consumed since the shock of Buildadeck's allegations was coffee and cigarettes. With the lack of food and sleep plus the intense anxiety my immune system had crashed. I'd acquired pneumonia and my doctor ordered me to stay in bed.

John travelled down to London for our High Court appearance with a note from the hospital to explain my absence. I was sure the judge would see the obvious truths of the matter. We could easily prove that everything we were being accused of was false.

Another important fact that was strongly in our favour was the Settlement Agreement that Nick had insisted we sign in May 2023. This was presented to us soon after we were both ousted as directors for allegedly stealing from the company and other trumped-up offences.

John and I were fired without notice from Buildadeck's board of directors on the 11th April 2023. I received a letter saying, "We have determined that you have committed gross misconduct during the course of your duties. We are therefore terminating your employment…"

Usually in cases like this you are suspended pending an investigation. What should have happened according to employment law is that we should have been suspended pending a full investigation. These findings should then have been presented to us and we should have been given the right of response. But for John and I there was no such procedure. When John informed Nick that what he was doing was illegal he replied, "I don't give a fuck about English Law."

Nick also told John and I that Buildadeck's investors had made the decision to fire us. After John asked for a copy of the minutes of that meeting Nick said he'd have to wait 30 days. Then John got an email saying the information was confidential. (We later heard from one of the attendees that the subject of my dismissal never came up during that meeting. Nick had told yet another lie.)

Nick was well aware of my mental health issues. Yet he'd said in a recorded call with John, "Don't think you can take the suicidal route out." I suspect he was also aware that the shock of potentially losing everything as well as the shame of it all would make me want to end my life.

John and I talked about the situation and he reluctantly agreed that we should walk away for the sake of my wellbeing. So I called Nick to discuss severing ties. I said that we wouldn't pursue any claim against the company if they dropped their threats to come after us.

During the call I told Nick I'd recorded a previous call where we'd discussed the payment of my deferred consideration and he had clearly given permission for me to draw the money in smaller amounts rather than all at once.

He went ballistic; shouting and swearing at me down the phone, telling me it was a criminal offence to record someone without their knowledge and that if I didn't delete it, he would report me to the police. I was scared to death, so I complied immediately. Unfortunately, in terms of the evidence we need now, it's too late.

Once I deleted the recording his whole demeanour changed instantly. I've never seen or heard anyone switch that fast. He went from devil to angel in the blink of an eye. John said his business partner at Safestyle used to do the same thing. It's a terror tactic coercive people use to immediately get what they want and most people will comply.

Nick agreed to give us each three-months' salary and pressured us to sign an agreement which stated we couldn't sue him for unfair dismissal or the £300,000 I was still owed for my installation companies.

The following text messages between me and Nick clearly show he was pushing me to sign this document and was losing patience with the involvement of our solicitors. He knew I was still reeling from shock, so he intensified the pressure.

20th April 2023
Me: "Hi Nick sorry to bother you. I thought we had an understanding that we wouldn't claim off you and you wouldn't claim off us. The drafts that have been sent through stop us from claiming whilst leaving you free to claim [against us]. Your solicitor has said that you won't entertain an agreement that stops you from claiming against us. As per our agreement please could you ask them to amend accordingly."

Nick: "We should speak... our lawyers pointed out some issues with a full release..."

25th April 2023
Nick: "Sharon... just confirming Joe received the revised docs late Friday."

Me: "Yes thanks, we spoke with him yesterday and he's reviewing. We told him we want it sorting out straight away."

Nick: "Thanks."

26th April 2023
Me: "We have gone through the documents with the solicitor today and he will be sending a couple of minor amendments for your review in the morning. There's nothing major because I don't want this dragging on and just want an end to it before John has his operation."

Nick: "Ok... will let them know."

2nd May 2023
Me: "Hi Nick, we still haven't received anything from your solicitors."

Nick: "Hi, people were away... should have comments today."

3rd May 2023
Me: "Hi Nick, our solicitors have responded to yours today. We have to take their advice. I wanted this to all be ended, but it doesn't look like this is possible unless you can influence your solicitors. As drafted it leaves with no guarantee we will get any money and it's all too upsetting."

Nick: "That's not true at all...I saw what your solicitors wrote and frankly their tone seemed pretty arrogant given what's gone on... I will speak with my counsel today...We want this done as well but I am not taking any nonsense."

Me: "All this is making me ill. You and I agreed you would have no claims against me and you would pay us three months' salary. I don't understand why the lawyers can't just produce a document that reflects that. If our lawyers came across as arrogant that's not a reflection of us. We just want to sign an agreement of what you and I agreed and get on with the rest of our lives."

Nick: "I agree and will sort it out. Here's the last point I am trying to resolve. Our due diligence reveals more bad behaviour regarding fancy cars and allowances... Our understanding was your prior car; a Porsche was in an accident and the insurance proceeds which should have gone to the company were instead used to buy your current Range Rover. You were also a director when this all occurred. If any of this is incorrect please let me know as I am trying to sort this out. These types of issues also [lead to] potential tax exposure please advise."

Me: "It's easier to put in an email to explain."

"The Porsche was bought in the company name but was always my car. I paid the £15,000 deposit and £500 per month, being the difference between my car allowance and the monthly payment. The car was supposed to be sold and the amount above the outstanding finance returned to me. However, one of the directors wanted to buy it so he took it for a couple of days to try it out.

Unfortunately, he had an accident and it was subsequently written off. The insurance paid off the outstanding finance and returned over £30,000 to the company which was technically mine. This was used to pay the deposit on the Range Rover, the balance of which is financed in my name.

If this had not been the case it would have been deducted from my deferred consideration. Every single transaction between me, the company and John has been recorded in the directors' loan account or the deferred consideration account and as you are aware there is still an outstanding balance over £300,000 due to me.

I am prepared to forgo any claim I may have to deferred consideration as I just want an end to it all… Hopefully we can all agree to just walk away with our arrangement and wish each other well."

Nick: "Thanks. Still in meetings; will read tonight."

4th May 2023
Me: "Hi Nick, money is more important than a car. Can we sign these papers before I lose everything?"

Nick: "I will let counsel know to wrap this up quickly."

Me: "Thank you."

5th May 2023
Nick: "I heard recently from my counsel that we were in agreement, now they just came back with additional requests. Just as I gave you my word above that we will make payment I am also giving you my word that if what we agree to above is not signed today we are

moving on and will start litigation to pursue all of our rights and remedies... This is in no way a threat as its unfortunately reality. Please advise as I am not wasting more monies on legal bills for this specific topic, thanks."

The conversation I had on the phone with him was even worse. I was crying as I tried to explain what he was doing was so wrong. He'd made us feel like criminals and we weren't. He was just a bully taking advantage of his power. I was shaking from fear and anxiety for days afterwards.

When we all signed those papers, Nick was well aware I had used money from my deferred consideration and knew that every payment I'd put through the company was clearly recorded and documented by Buildadeck's accounts department. But at the hearing in December 2023 our legal team failed to make it clear to the judge that this Settlement Agreement included the clause that no claims could be brought against me based on facts that were already known when it was signed.

The judge said he noted the existence of the agreement but couldn't determine its effect without clearer evidence. He also concluded that due to the nature of the allegations and the lack of available evidence there was a risk we might move or conceal our assets, so the freezing orders were granted. Although he did stress these were "interim protections" and he wasn't making any findings of fact or dishonesty.

These legal constraints are having a deeply damaging effect on our lives. We were being severely punished for something we hadn't done. All because on December 15th 2023, Buildadeck's barrister stood in front of the judge and even though she had sworn on oath, in my opinion she effectively committed perjury over and over again.

As you read this, there is still a freezing order on the sale of my house and our lives are literally on hold while Nick and his army of lawyers dangle us like puppets and torment us with brown envelopes full of official looking threats and false allegations, all numbered, capitalised and underlined.

I've been here before and regret not standing up against the terrorists and tyrants of this world. Having analysed everything in-depth and thanks to the support of a great team of therapists I no longer feel suicidal. I am determined to make my voice heard, clear my name and claim the damages I am rightfully owed.

Despite feeling enraged, intensely frustrated and isolated at times, I have to stay cool and logical or I won't have the strength to fight back. The question is, how much fight do I have left in me? I'm about to find out.

CHAPTER 6

Our Ex-Business Partner Stabs Us in the Back

When Nick and Commercide initially turned against us, our management team said they would stand with us and if one went, we all went. Some wrote letters of support, but only sent them to John. As many of them had school aged children, including Paul, we told them not to leave the company just because we were being forced out. They needed to stay for the sake of their families.

John had known Paul since he took over Buildadeck in 2016 and had given him his "big break" by suggesting he work with me and then mentoring him through his transition from fitter to installation director. Even after John's firing, they would call each other a couple of times a month and meet occasionally for a Costa coffee. This continued even after Nick had given Paul strict instructions to have no contact with him.

So you can imagine John's astonishment when he discovered Commercide's lawyer had produced a sworn affidavit from Paul at their freezing order application hearing on 15th December. In his statement Paul claimed to have had no knowledge of my building material purchases being offset against my deferred consideration.

In fact, he agreed with virtually everything John and I had been accused of. Ironically, he admitted he'd received his share of the deferred consideration, the very same thing I'd now been accused of "stealing!"

CAPITAL PUNISHMENT

After the hearing on the 21st of December 2023, John called him repeatedly. Each time Paul's phone was either switched off or went unanswered. Eventually John sent him a message saying if he didn't pick up, he'd have to drive over to his house because they needed to speak. This got an immediate reaction. Paul called him from a withheld number warning, "Don't you ever threaten to come to my house!" Eventually he calmed down and agreed to talk to him.

A few days after Christmas they met at a café about an hour away to avoid being spotted together. John told him how I'd taken the pills and that he'd tried to stop me and said if my liver had packed up, I'd only have lived for about a month.

John said, "I know she's threatened it before but this time she fucking did it. She's my world. I know she can be a pain, especially when she is under stress, but when she's on form, she's the sweetest, kindest, most generous person you could ever wish to meet."

Then he changed the subject and asked Paul why he'd signed a statement saying he knew nothing about the payments for the building materials.

"Well I didn't," he answered flatly.

John reminded him that there had been meetings between all three of us and not only had he agreed to the situation, he'd even sourced some of the materials and made the payments for them himself. He'd even asked another director to do the same thing. Why had he denied there had ever been any meetings about it?

John reminded him that the two of them had informal meetings virtually every day, usually just after 6:00am when they both arrived in the office.

In other meetings, the finance director would reconcile the accounts and then show the deferred consideration figure on the big screen in John's office. After this a list would appear of what I had spent on materials, exactly where the payments had gone and how much I had left in my "money owed to me" account.

John urged him, "You cannot leave it as it is. You need to tell them the truth that you knew about the payments. You need to tell them you were on the call with Nick when he agreed to paying the deferred consideration. And you need to tell them that you knew Buildadeck was buying stuff and Gary was keeping track of how much of it was left. They might be pissed now, but they are going to be really pissed when it gets to court and all this comes out."

Paul replied that one of Commercide's accountants had shoved a list of figures under his nose and asked what they were for. He'd replied that he didn't know. As for the meetings, he said he'd been asked if there were any records as to what was discussed. He'd told them notes had been taken, but not on a regular basis.

John also suggested to Paul that he needed to re-read his statement because it was all rubbish. Paul admitted this was true. Then he confessed that he knew he should have read it in detail but at the time he felt overwhelmed and pressured.

"It all happened so quick," he explained. "I had a 20-minute chat with the lawyer. Then he sent me a draft statement of what I'd said.

It was full of mistakes and they kept adding things I didn't say. I had to send it back six or seven times before I signed it,"

Then he added, "I've been kept in the dark. It's all been Commercide's people huddled in a corner. I didn't even know it had gone to court."

John told him that Buildadeck, on Commercide's instructions, had got a freezing order on me to stop me selling my house and that we were fast running out of money. Our legal costs just for that one day had cost us £20,000 and we were still fucked.

"What can I do about it?" he replied.

John said, "Tell them you got the text from Sharon and it upset you and made you think, so you re-read your statement and you're not happy with it. You need to read it again anyway because it's just not true."

Paul admitted, "I should really, but I'm shit at that type of thing. I mean to read it I'd just end up skimming through and saying, 'Yeah, it's fine,' instead of reading it word for word."

John reiterated, "You cannot leave your statement as it is and you have to tell the truth. Explain that you cannot lie and that it will look bad for everyone. Worst of all the company will spend a fortune on lawyers that it won't get back. Plus, it's a massive distraction from the work issues you've already got."

"I know the shit will hit the fan," Paul said, "Whether you want to or not you'll have to use all those recordings, messages and screenshots and whatever. To be honest I don't give a fuck… I was happier when I had my own deck fitting company and used to be able to take the kids to school on a morning, do a few jobs and be home for tea. I didn't have all this shit to deal with."

Paul told John he was due to speak to the Americans but wasn't sure when, but he did confirm he was going to put the record straight. John asked him to contact him after the call and tell him what was said. Paul said he'd let him know and they went their separate ways. A few of days later, after hearing nothing from him, John sent Paul a text message:

"Hi mate, sorry to bug you… This is doing my head in. Is there any chance you could sort this out before you go away on holiday. Could you send me something confirming you knew about the payments so I can at least have something to work with whilst you're away."

Paul's last message to him is as follows:

John, I cannot believe you have sent this text to me. This is now harassment and also threatening behaviour as per previous texts, emails and calls. Sharon sending me that text is a threat to me. You saying you will come to my house because I didn't text back is a threat to me and my family. I will now take legal advice moving forwards."

I can forgive Paul for lying about knowing my land and the materials I'd purchased through Buildadeck were all legitimate, documented transactions that were known to the directors. He was protecting himself so he could provide for his family.

He had no choice but to withdraw from us so he didn't have to think about how badly he'd betrayed us. No doubt he will have suffered. Guilt is a powerful emotion. So, in some ways he is also another victim of Commercide's ruthlessness and greed.

CHAPTER 7

How I Became a Part of the Buildadeck Family

After "Dragons' Den," writing my book "Mother of Invention" and doing the public speaking circuit I lost the interest in being self-employed. I thought the routine of a regular job would help me move on from the stress of my experience with the investors from the TV show.

I was all too familiar with investment companies' dirty tactics and how they exploited other people's trust and hard work to get their hands on as much money as they could. This is why I'd had my doubts about Commercide from the start.

Because I couldn't face going through anything like this again, in 2014 I took a job as sales director at a building materials supplier called Mavil Supplies in Hull. Its owner was someone I'd known for years. The company's core business was windows but it also supplied UPVC decking.

After a year, the owner told me to stop selling and slow down because all the business I was bringing in had maxed out his credit with his supply chain. It had reached the point where his business was at risk. Basically, I was making more sales than the company could handle and putting too much pressure on the company's cash flow.

During this time, I'd never lost touch with John, who'd been a very good friend since my "Dragons' Den" days. He was my confidante and I was his. We would often meet for dinner and give each other support and advice. I was aware of all the problems he had gone through with his partner at Safestyle and he'd tell me how his legal action was progressing.

He'd just acquired two companies: LUPA Windows and Buildadeck Fencing and Decking UK with £15 million in funding from Commercide Ventures in 2016. This funding was provided purely as a loan. Commercide did not have a shareholding in either of these companies as is common with this type of capital investment firm.

Outdoor decking made from longer lasting alternatives to wood was a new idea and a largely untapped market in the UK. Because I'd exhausted my potential at Mavil Supplies, John encouraged me to start my own business alongside his. I didn't want to stretch my finances too far, so I joined forces with one of Mavil Supplies' customers, a guy called Jim who built lodges. Before doing so I did ask my former boss for permission to take his account and supply him with materials direct.

In 2016 Jim and I formed a decking company together. Jim employed a lot of staff, which was costly due to the unpredictable nature of the business. To save money, I worked out of his industrial unit and hired staff from an agency when they were needed. This reduced his overheads dramatically. The idea was that I'd pay his full-time guys when they did work for me, and when they weren't needed Jim paid their salary. It was an arrangement that worked well for both of us.

Mavil Supplies' window manufacturer let me buy at the same price as them so I could sell to the lodge industry. The profit I made on the windows allowed me to pay myself a wage. Of course, I brought in so much business from "The Lawns Show" (the annual lodge and caravan exhibition) our decking business quickly took off. I built contacts fast and could see the business had huge potential.

To ease the pressure on cash flow I was buying materials from Mavil's supplier and some from John. Having two suppliers was ideal because it meant I could grow the business on credit until my customers paid me.

Over those first few months I spent a lot of time with John. This is when our relationship changed and we developed feelings for each other. He helped me understand and accept the traumas I'd been through and was business-minded like me. We had so much in common it was uncanny. We were just meant to be together.

As my business grew, I came to realise that Jim had a very bad reputation in the industry. His after sales service was shocking. People would turn up at the unit complaining and demanding that their projects were completed or re-done. His staff weren't doing their jobs properly and needed to learn how to build the decks to a better standard, so I took them over to John's company Buildadeck for training. They had the best reputation in the field and could teach Jim's guys how to install properly.

However, after getting this training Jim told his guys to work in their usual way, going against everything they'd just learned. Because the installers were paid by Jim, they had no choice but to listen to him and not me. I was fuming. This was my business and Jim was supposed to be a silent partner. Realising his work ethic was not the same as mine and hearing the negative feedback from his customers, I already had serious doubts that we could continue to work together, but this was the final straw.

John knew a deck installer called Paul who bought materials from him and asked him to help me repair the damage Jim's guys had done. He saved the deck and my reputation. Luckily, the client never got to see the stress I had to go through to put the job right.

Paul was impressed by the number of contacts I'd built up in a short period of time and how many projects we had in the pipeline. He later told me that he wished he was in business with me and said to one of his friends, "There's something about Sharon. She's got her head screwed on."

John knew that having access to the end user market would be a way of growing Buildadeck Fencing and Decking. To prove this theory he suggested that he, Paul and myself went into business together. We formed a new company called Buildadeck East Coast and agreed that it would be treated the same way as all other approved installers. To have given it preferential treatment would not have allowed us to prove the concept.

The initial agreement was John and I would hold a 40% stake each and Paul the other 20%. John said it would look better for the company to be seen as totally independent from his, so I held his share, which meant that on paper it looked like I had an 80% stake in the company. I was happy to forfeit a wage in the early days, which is the same for almost every entrepreneur who goes on to be a success.

Paul wanted to continue with his own business until he felt comfortable about integrating it into this new venture. He couldn't afford to take a temporary drop in income because he had a family to support.

The decking around a lodge or caravan is a luxury people are prepared to pay for because of the amount of extra outdoor space it provides in all weathers. But when you're spending thousands, you expect to get an excellent product installed properly and without delay. Our competitor's lead times were between three and six weeks. Some were even longer, depending on the time of year. Plus, there were other failings in the industry that we could turn to our advantage.

Because all decking materials and deck designs are pretty much the same, Buildadeck East Coast had to be different to stand out from the rest. So I suggested that we should promote the fact that we provided a fitting time within seven working days. A fast, professional service would be our unique selling point (USP) and give us a competitive advantage.

Thankfully, Paul had chosen his fitters wisely so he knew how to work quickly. For example, the competition took two days to build a wrap-around deck, but Paul had figured out how to achieve the same results within a day. Because of this we could pass our labour cost saving onto the customer, making our decks cheaper than anyone else's. Now we had two USPs! Business is easy when you are passionate about being the best.

Another failing of our competition was poor aftersales service. There were many times that lodge resort sales managers would tell me their customers were hounding them about simple little niggles and complaints.

One of our competitors was known for taking six months to do remedial work. This was probably due to the fact that the holiday parks they worked with were mostly run by the older semi-retired generation who just wanted a quiet life, so
they either ignored any complaints or were just too overwhelmed to deal with them.

We decided to commit to doing any remedial work within 48 hours. So now we had three USPs. This is the magic number that guarantees success! Within days of promoting our superior business model we were inundated with orders.

Paul assured me he would never let me down when it came to maintaining high standards or meeting lead times. In return I promised to keep the orders pipeline flowing. We didn't want to be known for employing seasonal staff, so we committed to paying a full-time workforce regardless of the amount of business. We were both under pressure to perform, but because of our set goals it worked.

I remember our first argument. I had secured business in so many parks that Paul said we needed to extend our lead time. I insisted we couldn't change our proposition because that's what gave us the edge. We were both at a stalemate and John had to step it to settle things.

I remember that meeting in a pub garden like it was yesterday. John reminded us both of the commitments and promises we'd made to each other and explained that it was a nice problem to have. He said it was never going to be easy and we had to find a way to deliver on our promises or we'd lose all credibility and be like all the rest.

By the morning Paul had come up with a plan. He had strong workers who could do installations in their sleep. If he split his teams so there was one of these leaders in each group and hired two trainees it might work. It did. We grew at even greater speed and smashed the industry on its head.

Two of our competitors even came to our exhibition stand the following year and congratulated us on our success. They said we had set standards that were almost impossible to beat. Nobody could touch us on service or price.

We then had the opportunity to duplicate our business model in the South of England. I thought it was too early to take on another responsibility so far away. I was worried that if we took our eye off our baby we would jeopardise what we'd already built. We took the plunge and did it anyway. We learned different lessons with that journey, but the core principles of our business model were repeated and our winning formula was a success.

John saw how we operated and admired what we'd achieved. I recall that he said he saw something in me the very first time we met, saying, "You remind me so much of Mitu Misra (his former business partner at Safestyle UK) with your drive and tenacity, but fortunately you don't have any of his nasty qualities."

He told me that throughout history there had been a unique set of circumstances that brought people together with amazing results. Apparently, he thought Paul and I were another Rolls and Royce or Marks and Spencer!

John knew there was more profit to be had if his company not only supplied decking but installed it too. He speculated that if he bought Paul and myself out, Buildadeck Fencing and Decking UK would see a good return on the investment. Plus, John and I knew we'd work well together.

So, he approached Commercide's CEO and founder, Nick Smith, for an additional loan to buy out selected Buildadeck-approved installers. Commercide was 100% behind the idea and offered to lend him another £5 million to cover the purchase of Buildadeck East Coast for £2.2 million, with additional funds to buy out two other installation companies.

We waited for months while Commercide investigated everything from our accounts and our working methods to our personalities, lifestyles and health. Nick then told John they'd seen a post of us on Facebook and he was furious he'd never told him we were in a relationship. After this he withdrew his offer of funding.

John couldn't understand what difference it made. I felt it was an insult to me because it seemed they assumed John was bringing me onboard as a favour. After all their background research, didn't they see I'd been an entrepreneur and a successful businesswoman for decades and had founded my own successful decking company?

It was me who'd done all the hard work getting all the holiday park owners to believe in us when Buildadeck East Coast was starting out. And it was also mainly due to my hard work and commitment that our installation companies delivered on every promise we made to our customers.

I was fuming and demanded to speak to Nick myself. I've always been clear and honest with people, possibly because I have ADHD and cannot tolerate time wasters or bullshitters. Plus, diplomacy is not my strongest point because I believe in action not words. So, I imagine Nick was quite stunned when I updated him on my history of accomplishments.

He must have understood the fire in my belly because soon after our conversation he confirmed that Commercide would continue with the acquisition of Buildadeck East Coast and the other approved installers.

The due diligence process was stressful and prolonged. Paul and I were interviewed in-depth by the auditors. We had to present our plans for future growth and give them all our projections. My plan was to go international and Cyprus was going to be our first test. I have always had big dreams and will always reach for the stars!

Being an empath, I did feel bad that Paul wouldn't receive as much as me due to our original agreement and told him that going forward it would be 50/50, and eventually it was.

Paul and I were led to believe that Commercide would give us around 70% of the value of our business on day one and the rest would be paid dependent upon meeting performance targets. But a week before we were due to agree to their offer and sign the paperwork, John informed us that Commercide's terms had changed.

Nick said they would honour their offer, but the consideration (the agreed sale price) due to Buildadeck's approved installers would be paid from Buildadeck Fencing and Decking's own funds.

Knowing that this wasn't possible, Nick said he would give us a third of money on signing. We would receive a third a year later which would be paid out of Buildadeck's profits and the final third a year after that, providing we met Commercide's targets.

Paul and I were shocked and angry. I told John I didn't trust Nick as far as I could throw him and we should just carry on as separate companies without Commercide's involvement. Paul said he'd go with whatever I decided. But when I saw the disappointment in his eyes I knew I couldn't live with that.

My heart told me to walk away, but my head told me Paul would never forgive me for taking away his chance of a payout and his resentment would probably break our working relationship. In October 2018, shortly after Nick presented his much-reduced offer, against my better judgement we signed off on the deal.

Commercide's withdrawal of the £5 million facility meant the £2.2 million for Buildadeck East Coast would have to be made in stage payments. We signed the papers in Leeds and were euphoric. Paul and I were given shares of Buildadeck UK as well as private healthcare, a generous car allowance and a fantastic salary.

Buildadeck's approved installers also had the choice to cash out and one chose to do so, so on the same day we acquired another approved installer in the North East. The owner of the business had been ill and he and his wife wanted to take early retirement.

The other approved installers, having seen the buy-outs that had been done, became greedy. They wrongly believed their companies were worth considerably more than mine. When we refused to meet their unrealistic demands, they took their business elsewhere.

Not to be defeated, one by one as each new area became available, we duplicated our winning formula and Buildadeck's reputation as a premium one-stop deck company was secured.

But despite all this growth and success, the fact that Nick had moved the goal posts and changed the original deal didn't sit well with me. My gut was telling me that we'd just made a huge mistake. I have regretted not following my instincts since the day we signed that contract.

CAPITAL PUNISHMENT

CHAPTER 8

The Rot Sets In

Over the following year, Nick would hold conference calls and speak to us on a regular basis. I was struck by something he said during one of these briefings. He'd been angry the previous time John and I had spoken to him and had apologised saying, "If I come across as being in a bad mood it's because I'm trying to get the sale of one of my other investments over the line and the owner of the business is a thieving robbing bastard." This was the first time I experienced the ruthless, foul-mouthed side of Nick.

A few months later the same scenario repeated itself. I told John and Paul about Nick's hostile manner towards his clients and that I sensed trouble ahead. Was this one of Nick's tried and tested tactics? He would pull funding in order to force the sale of a business, accuse the owners of theft and then sue them for everything they had?

A year had passed and it was time to collect our second chunk of money. Nick called John and told him to meet with him and a member of his European team at a hotel in London. Immediately I told Paul, "We're not getting our money." I was right.

Nick told us that despite Buildadeck's growth, its profits had been used to expand the business so there wasn't enough left to pay us. He said, "We would appreciate a delay on the payment of the first deferred consideration until cash flow allows. Then you'll be paid 8% per annum on what you're owed."

The words, "Fuck you!" came to mind. He knew he had us over a barrel. What were we going to do? We'd put our hearts and souls into this business and couldn't just walk away. I just had to accept the situation.

Taking the pragmatic view, we had no immediate need for the money and would only have put it in the bank which was paying 8% anyway, so we reluctantly accepted his offer. We went back to South Yorkshire feeling very deflated. I wasn't going to say the words "I told you so," because that would have achieved nothing.

The next day, we all met early in the morning and tried to make light of the situation to motivate ourselves to keep going. John and I buried ourselves in work. Our life experiences had been similar and we viewed running a business as something of a therapy and an escape. Having been deprived of support growing up, we made up for it by spending every hour we had grafting to create a better future for ourselves.

Paul didn't work the hours we did. He had his priorities right. He now worked from 9 to 5 most days because his family came first. At times this irritated me, but realistically it was me and John who had it all wrong.

During this time John was also dealing with his litigation case with Safestyle UK (which I'll explain more about in the next chapter). Shockingly, he lost. Not satisfied with keeping £77 million from the sale of Safestyle UK, his ex-business partner of 20 plus years handed him a bill of £1.8m for legal fees which had to be settled within 28 days. Even if he had the money John still wouldn't have paid. Consequently, he was made bankrupt in June 2019.

CAPITAL PUNISHMENT

Nick had told us that if John was made bankrupt, he would have to be removed as the CEO and director. He called for a meeting and informed us that a financial expert would have to be brought in.

Using the authorities that were detailed in the documents John had signed, Nick took control of Buildadeck and LUPA Windows, with Commercide assuming John's 70% shareholding and Paul and myself retaining 14% each. All of this was done with Nick's promise to John that he was not looking "to steal" his shares and they would be returned to him when the time was right. In addition, he insisted that John stayed on in an advisory capacity.

John had no choice in the matter because being bankrupt prevented him from being a director of a UK company. Consequently, he had to resign. I was appointed CEO and being a control freak I also insisted on keeping my role of sales director, which meant I put enormous pressure on myself.

Our customers were informed of the situation and because we were upfront about everything John's departure didn't affect the business in any way. They all knew about John's legal woes and were aware that the situation wasn't his fault. Plus, he was still involved with the running of the company, albeit in a less official way.

In 2020 we had the Covid lockdowns to contend with. Because we were technically 70 % owned by an American company, we were not entitled to any UK relief funding. So Commercide agreed that our interest payments could be suspended and any loan payments we made would be offset against the principal debt.

It was shortly after this that Nick announced he wanted to sell or refinance Buildadeck because the repayment date for the loan had passed. It all started off quite amicably but then Nick instructed an accountancy firm to manage the process. John and this consultant immediately took a dislike to each other. This was primarily due to the auditor's inflated valuation of £30 million for the company, which seemed ridiculous to John.

In 2022 as we prepared for selling the business, we were interested to know how any proceeds from the sale would be split and asked Nick for a legal agreement. He finally agreed to this and had his lawyers draw up contracts. The agreement stated that after the debt had been paid off, the surplus would be paid to myself and Paul. But the key issue was still this figure of what the actual outstanding debt owed to Commercide was.

Nick refused to state a number, saying it would be whatever it was on the day. Our solicitor pushed back on this because leaving it open meant it could be anything. They could even state it as being more than any sale price!

(John's original loan to buy LUPA Windows and Buildadeck ran from 2016 to 2021. At the time LUPA was the biggest of the two companies with a £16 million turnover against Buildadeck's £6 million. When LUPA went into administration in 2020 a proportionate amount of the debt should have been attributed to LUPA (roughly two thirds) and written off. We never know if this happened, but it would have made sense.)

In September 2022, Buildadeck's accounts stated this debt as being just over £13.5 million. Nick quoted a figure of £18 million, presumably having added all kinds of additional late payment fees.

When John refused to accept Buildadeck's debt figure would be "flexible," Nick emailed him back saying, "Your lawyer is trying to over-negotiate the agreement. It's not open for further negotiation as we already discussed the details. This is taking up time and money. Let me know by tonight if you're signing as is or we all get on a call and discuss who manages the company going forward. I'm tired of this back and forth."

John took that to mean sign or you are sacked! Because he knew he'd have more control inside the company than outside, he reluctantly signed the document.

Unhappy with the direction in which things were going, John began looking for other investors to pay Commercide off. Nick's consultant didn't like this because independent valuations were coming in at far less than the £30 million he'd pulled out of the air. Instead, initial interest suggested a valuation around the £20 million mark. Ultimately, two offers came back at £16 million and £17 million.

Had Buildadeck's debt been £13.5 million as stated in the audited accounts, the shareholders would probably have accepted the highest offer which would have given us a surplus of £3.5 million. But as Nick had estimated the debt to be £18 million, which was less than the highest bid, he had the right to refuse the offer, which he did.

The consultant told Nick that John was trying to sabotage the sale process and steal his business back "on the cheap." When Nick heard about the low valuations, he was incandescent with rage and started a smear campaign against John, accusing him of being a dishonest, greedy cheat.

He couldn't sack him for under-performing because he'd taken the business to £24 million, making £4 million a year before interest, taxes and depreciation, so he had to come up with something else. Due to the fact that not everything was officially documented at Buildadeck (Nick avoided written records and preferred to conduct business with conference calls) he focused on "unauthorised payments."

With John technically being the majority shareholder, he didn't need authorisation to make payments. Unfortunately, Commercide's documentation showed otherwise after John's wholly unfair mislabelling as being bankrupt. With Commercide holding his 70% shareholding, John now needed authorisation for a lot of things and appeared to owe them a fiduciary duty. This meant he was legally obligated to act in their best interests and not his own.

To back up their argument it was claimed that John paid my deferred consideration when it was not due and bought building materials through the company on my behalf. Commercide also states in their lawsuit that John did this when the company was struggling and not paying HMRC or the interest on their loan. They accused him of favouring me over Buildadeck's other creditors.

Not only that, Commercide are now portraying themselves as the victim, saying they had trusted us to run the business and this trust was not rewarded. Their investment was not a successful one and they had suffered "substantial losses" from which they were still recovering. All of this is categorically untrue. The profits we were generating while we were there are proof of this.

The final independently audited accounts for when John was CEO show turnover was up from £15 million to £24 million, gross profits were up from £5 million to £10 million. The amount the company owed to Commercide also dropped from £14.4 million in 2021 to £13.6 million in 2022. In other words, in 2022 Buildadeck reduced its loan by £800,000 and paid Commercide £1.2 million in interest.

It is true there were liabilities to HMRC. As with most companies the pandemic led to all sorts of cash issues, but these were debts due from 2022 and everyone was getting paid. Paul and I had been owed £1.4 million since 2019 and 2020, making ours Buildadeck's oldest debt. Yet John still didn't pay it all off. He paid it off bit by bit, in line with any other creditor.

It's only when a company becomes insolvent, which Buildadeck definitely was not, that the responsibility of a director switches to that of its creditors. So yes, John takes great umbrage at the suggestion he paid me when the company was struggling. This is simply not the case and the accounts clearly show that.

Immediately after John left, the business took a massive turn for the worse, Sales fell and costs spiralled. Nick was beginning to look foolish for ousting him. In order to save face and recoup their self-inflicted losses, a plan was hatched to bring a claim against John.

Nick asserted that he had no choice but to let him go because he'd been cheating on his expenses. How could he keep him on when he'd stolen so much from the company?

Because John had been made bankrupt after losing a lawsuit against his former business partner he knew he'd get nothing from suing him. But I owned a house worth £2 million. So, they conspired to contrive a litany of groundless claims against me instead. It was just pure, money-grabbing greed.

CAPITAL PUNISHMENT

CHAPTER 9

How John Was "Framed"

My husband, John Ross was born in Leeds in 1965. The youngest of four children, he was the result of his mother's 10-year-long affair with a married man he'd never met. He hated his father for abandoning him and could never understand why he would spend time with his other kids but not him. His mother later told him she had kept them apart, which was something he never forgave.

John had always worked from a very young age and loved it. Having money felt like a superpower. In his teens he realised that it also brought happiness to others. Since then, he has always wondered if that's where its real value lies.

Because of this he's always strived to make money for others, paid the best wages and given money to good causes. He has also invested in other people to help them achieve their goals and has probably been instrumental in making at least half a dozen millionaires. At this tough time of his life he sometimes wonders where are they now?

In 1985 John was an independent financial advisor selling insurance policies. One fateful day a representative, an Indian guy called Mitu who worked for another insurance company, visited his office to obtain car insurance. He asked to speak to someone about arranging a mortgage and was referred to John.

The two formed an informal partnership that brought Mitu's house buying clients and John's mortgage lenders together. No money was shared or exchanged between them. John took a fee from the lender and Mitu took fees from his clients. They continued working like this together amicably but rarely socialised.

Towards the end of 1992, Mitu told John there was a lot of money to be made in double glazing, but only if you had your own company. So, in December 1992 John and Mitu formed Safestyle UK. Due to a previous bankruptcy, Mitu insisted that John held all the shares as by law Mitu was not allowed to have a significant interest in any company.

The business grew rapidly and eventually became the largest replacement window company in the UK.

Everything derogatory that has ever been said about double glazing sales is probably true. In those early days it was a horrible business where the worst degenerates of society could earn a lot of money without any regard for whether the homeowner could afford new windows. This never sat well with John and given what later transpired, he sometimes wonders if he got what he deserved.

Mitu and John had clearly defined roles. Mitu brought in the sales and John did everything else. The standing Joke was that "Fat Rossy" ran the "sane department" while Mitu and his team acted like they were on a permanent bachelor weekend.

As the business developed, Mitu decided it was time he was recognised as a shareholder. They had always agreed that John owned 37.5% of the company and Mitu 62.5%. This was how things officially stood until the Office of Fair Trading (OFT) launched an investigation and took the company's consumer credit licence away. Over half of all sales were sold on finance, so without the licence the business would have suffered tremendously.

After spending £1 million on legal fees, the OFT's decision was overturned. John had convinced them that he would run the business and Mitu would have no say in the control of the company. This resulted in John once again appearing to be the 100% owner of Safestyle.

There was a sea change at the company and Safestyle cleaned up their act. By 2005 John had recruited and developed a management team that was so competent that he and Mitu only visited the office around once a week.

He had also begun to develop a property portfolio and was investing in start-up and established businesses including a media agency, asset management company, a recruitment company, restaurant and software business. He was even listed in "42 under 42" and the Sunday Times Rich List (although he says their figures were wrong!).

It was around this time that John and I first met. He was still married at the time. I had approached him to invest in my magnetic cable threading tool invention. John later told me that he saw more potential in me than he did my "Magnamole" product which was a plastic rod with magnets at both ends that pulls cables through cavity walls. He said I had all of Mitu's drive and enthusiasm but without the lying and cheating.

A few months later, in 2008, John had a large benign tumour removed from his pelvic cavity. He was expected to stay in hospital for about five nights, but during the surgery his femoral artery was accidentally severed and couldn't be stitched back together. He needed 16 pints of blood (which is the record for that hospital for anyone having elective surgery) and was put into an induced coma. His family was told if anyone wanted to see him, they had best get there quick because he wouldn't make it through the night.

As a result of the massive blood loss, John suffered "compartment syndrome" and was rushed back to the operating theatre where fasciotomies were carried out on both sides of his lower legs. In simple terms, the surgeon cut his legs open to drain the toxins and remove any dying muscle tissue.

In addition to spending 13 days in a coma, he also had complete kidney failure. He'd caught MRSA and had a Clostridioide difficile colon infection (C-Diff for short) and spent four months in isolation. The doctors told him he would never walk again. All these serious health problems meant he was away from Safestyle for about a year. While there was an option agreement for Mitu to buy the company back from his estate in the event of his death, this scenario was never discussed.

When John returned to Safestyle in 2008, he discovered the business had been badly affected by the credit crunch. Unfortunately, due to his severely weakened physical state he was no longer able to deal with these new challenges

By now, Safestyle was in breach of its covenants with the bank which had loaned the company several million pounds. So, John told me that Mitu and his accountants came up with a scheme to write off some of the debt and engaged a specialist firm of accountants to present their case. However, the bank refused to play ball and pushed for the sale of the company. Due to John's incapacitation, the bank initiated an accelerated sale through another accountancy firm and a private equity company bid £16 million for Safestyle.

Worried that the bank might appoint administrators, Mitu and John attempted to stall the sale. It was at this point that Mitu said John should transfer all his shares to him. Having held Mitu's shares for many years John presumed Mitu would do the same and revert to the original division of shares when required.

Mitu paid John £1 for Safestyle – including its bank debt – and assured him that their beneficial ownership structure of 62.5% and 37.5% would remain.

Shortly after "buying" the company Mitu told John to leave without any additional financial compensation. Even his consultancy fee was reduced. And in lieu of his 37.5% he was offered a 10% shareholding provided he "behaved himself."

John then discovered that Safestyle was being prepared for flotation on the stock market. In his opinion his exclusion was strategic. He met with Safestyle's senior management team who all agreed that he had been treated outrageously, but they were powerless to do anything.

In 2013 Safestyle was floated on the London Alternative investment market for £77 million with its now perceived sole "founder" Mitu receiving the entire value in cash. John was hit by a myriad of emotions and questions of "why, what and when?" and wondered if he would ever get his rightful share of the proceeds? He had turned down Mitu's 10% offer as it did not reflect the large extent to which he had helped build the business.

He remembers sitting on the floor watching his youngest son Joseph playing when his phone rang. It was Mitu. John said "Hello" and Mitu replied, "There is not a day since you left that I have not thought about you. The only way I will ever be free of you is to make sure you don't get another penny…You're getting fuck all!"

Then he hung up. John called him straight back but Mitu had immediately blocked him. He tried to contact Mitu again but without success. He couldn't believe it. This was treachery at an inconceivable level. John realised he had never really known the real Mitu in all the decades they'd worked together.

A few days later, Mitu's assistant Steve called to say that Mitu would meet with him at a hotel on the outskirts of Bradford to discuss the matter. John turned up early and waited in the foyer. Half an hour past the meeting time there was no sign of Mitu. He was about to leave when Steve walked in. He explained that Mitu would not be coming but he was prepared to give him £1 million as a full and final settlement if he went away quietly.

Insulted by the offer John told Steve he was owed £29 million. As Mitu's previous offer of 10% of the sale price of £7 million had been unacceptable, he would certainly not be agreeing to take £1 million.

John had no choice but to contact a lawyer and initiate a lawsuit against Mitu. Such was the strength of his case John's law firm agreed to act on a contingent fee, meaning he only had to pay for disbursements. When they won the lawyers would be entitled to a bonus of up to double their normal fee.

Initially the case did not seem overly complicated, but as often happens with litigation, the whole thing began to spiral out of control. In all, the case took over five years to be heard and John spent two weeks at the High Court in London presenting the details of his dealings with Mitu.

The burning question was why would anyone transfer a multi-million-pound asset like Safestyle shares (worth at least £30 million) to someone else for £1 unless there was some other agreement between the parties?

During his testimony on the witness stand Mitu said the offer of £1 million made by Steve was intended to be the starting point for negotiations. Obviously, he knew John was due a considerable sum from the sale of Safestyle. However, in court John had to prove on the balance of probability what the exact terms of the agreement between himself and Mitu had been. By now, Mitu was denying any kind of deal had ever been made.

Without physical evidence, John was unable to prove the percentage of shareholdings that had been agreed, so the judge had no choice but to rule against him.

CAPITAL PUNISHMENT

CHAPTER 10

How This Litigation Has Changed John

What happened to John in 2023 with Buildadeck UK was different. It was nothing compared to Safestyle in monetary terms, but the whole experience killed him inside. This time he truly felt he had lost it all. He was just existing from one day to the next, with no ambition, no desire for his name in lights or the buzz of business. He had nothing to look forward to.

John had dealt with so many negative situations over the years and now had ample time to reflect on them and ask himself why he'd been so unlucky. Was it just him? Maybe he'd got everything wrong.

Being the CEO of a private company is a lonely place to be. Everyone wants a piece of you. People you have nothing in common with want to be your friend. Everyone comes to you with their problems, unless they're drunk, in which case it's, "Do you know what I would do if I were you?"

As he became more successful with Safestyle, assuming success is measured in material things, the lonelier he became. He was fortunate enough to buy a farm and that became his solace. It was the one place he was truly happy.

Even though he had a fleet of luxury cars, including two Ferrari's, he just wanted to be alone on his farm with his two German shepherds: Barca (named by his son Damian after Barcelona football club) and Raul (named by his other son

Dominic after his favourite player at Real Madrid). All they wanted from him was food and affection and in return they loved him unconditionally.

The problem was, he didn't spend enough time there. He had to be part of the rat race. It was like a drug. Even though he hated it, he couldn't live without it. It became a vicious circle. When he was at home he needed to be at work and when he was at work he needed to be in the pub. Then after 14 hours sat boozing, he needed to be at home. Incidentally, he never drank at home so he didn't consider himself to be an alcoholic, but he believes he wasn't far off.

He doesn't really know how he got to being such a big drinker, but looking back he thinks it was an escape mechanism. It allowed him to abandon his personal responsibilities when he was employing hundreds of people and their livelihoods were resting on his every decision.

John considers himself as being quite an intelligent person with an ability for problem solving. In his youth he was extremely confident, funny and nice to be around, but now he avoids socialising and social events in general.

Being manipulated by Mitu – who he considered to be a trusted friend – for so many years is a major contributing factor in this. His long, isolated hospital stay is another. And of course, losing everything on top has led him to become quite introverted and contemplative.

As a young man he was always fighting, getting suspended from school and getting into trouble with the police. But as he grew up, he simply learned to avoid confrontation when he thought it would be unproductive.

He thought that by stepping back he was choosing wisdom over conflict. But looking back, he realises that he went too far the other way and has been taken advantage of, not just to his own detriment, but to the detriment of those he should have stood up for and protected.

He told himself he was choosing his battles wisely, but in reality, he was letting injustices slide and trusting that truth and fairness would prevail. But it didn't. Because fairness isn't something that just happens. It's something you have to fight for.

Perhaps in avoiding confrontation for so long he had unintentionally taught himself to fear it. Now he sees that avoiding conflict isn't wisdom. It's a slow surrender and a habit that evolves until standing up for yourself feels uncomfortable and even daunting.

Confrontation often isn't about aggression; it's about having the courage to say, "This is not right," or "This is not okay." It's about drawing the line even when it's uncomfortable, or feels like it's too late. John now says the real damage isn't in the battles we fight. It's in the ones we should have fought and didn't. He swears he will never make that mistake again.

The other thing that has taken him a long time to realise is that money doesn't make anyone happy and striving for happiness in itself can be self-defeating. Peace of mind is far more important, even if it means you have to fight for it.

CHAPTER 11

TikTok World

I was desperate for someone to publicise our story. I needed everyone to know how I had falsely been accused of stealing from the company and how Commercide Ventures and its CEO Nick Smith had weaponised the legal system against us. Their claims were so outrageous they would send anyone crazy with disbelief.

They were so good at obfuscating the facts, lying and maintaining their accusations of wrongdoing I was scared they might convince everyone that they were the victims in all of this and not us. I was eager to make the true versions of events known.

During all this turmoil I couldn't watch TV. I couldn't sleep and life became very lonely. Somehow, I found myself drawn into the TikTok world. It was a lively light-hearted distraction from the dark and heavy subject of our legal battle. Other people's dramas got my attention and Tik Tok became my virtual social life.

I admired the commitment and the hours some content creators dedicated to it. They had thousands of views, but were clearly struggling and living day to day. They were like worker bees continually striving to create a buzz. What I also noticed was they tended to have narcissistic, manipulative traits. It made me question the psychology of those who chased success, including myself.

Strangely enough, all the bullying, trolling and weirdos you find on this platform diverted me away from all the misery and horrors in my own life and gave me a break from the rage I felt towards Nick and his team at Commercide Ventures.

In a bizarre coincidence (or was it?) one of the first people that reached out to me was a woman who had once worked in James Caan's office. Caan was the "Dragons' Den" investor who tried to take over my company by getting me to sign a misleading contract. What were the chances of someone related to him getting in touch with me almost on the same day I joined the platform?

She said she remembered me from my "Dragons' Den" days and was surprised to hear from her colleagues that I'd pulled out of my agreement with James. She told me he'd moved to Monaco and she was no longer had contact with him.

She was using TikTok to promote an American-made detox product that removed heavy metals from the body and wanted to know how to make her video go viral. I told her to respond to every comment even if it was a troll because they drive the traffic.

After our exchange she sent me a sample in the post and said I needed to take one drop per day at night time and that I'd get bad headaches and probably feel sick initially. She called me every day to see if I had a reaction to it. I lied and said I was fine. It hadn't given me headaches because I didn't take it. Who knows what the stuff was.

I didn't hear from her again until I posted a video detailing all the lies and bullying I'd been subjected to by Commercide and how I was going to write a book about it. I checked her stream to see how her business was going and was surprised she was just reposting other people's videos. Then she sent me a message asking if I wanted to chat.

Why was she suddenly interested when I mentioned my legal troubles? Was James behind this? Or even Commercide? Yes, I was becoming paranoid, but I still thought it was odd that this woman had contacted me, so I ghosted her. Thankfully, TikTok was full of distractions and it wasn't long before my attention was diverted by a disturbing situation.

A character called Piadro was receiving a lot of hate. One of his followers had committed suicide and everyone blamed him and a girl called Joker for her death. Piadro took no responsibility for his part in driving this poor woman to suicide. She'd been sending them both money in the form of "lions" which cost hundreds of pounds. When she jumped into their chat you could clearly see and hear that she'd been drinking.

Because I was new to TikTok and didn't know the back story I joined the tide of people who were trolling Piadro and Joker. I didn't say anything too harsh, just the odd suggestion that they should give this poor woman her money back or at least send it to her family.

A few days later I saw Joker have her own personal crisis and felt awful. I'd sent her a message telling her she was acting horrendously and her attitude wasn't nice to watch. When she appeared to be constantly in tears I really did feel for her. She took all the attacks to heart and had also started abusing alcohol.

I was ashamed I'd sent that nasty message and analysed my reaction. Why was I so upset? Why did I cry at the sight of her tears? Because I felt her pain. It reminded me of all the terrible accusations that had been made against me. Why were John and I reliving the horrors from our past like a Matrix film?

Because Joker didn't receive many messages, she started interacting with me every day and I'd say something supportive. I'd started seeing a hospital therapist and wanted Joker to see her too. I spoke to John and he agreed helping her was a good thing to do, so she had a few sessions paid for by me.

Then she started calling me saying she needed a deposit for a house. I said if I had the money I would have given it to her. Then after I criticised her for getting upset about a guy she'd met online but not in person, she blocked me. I guess I was no longer of use. I was out of my depth trying to be a good Samaritan to someone I'd never met and vowed never to fall into that trap again.

I told my therapist about my new TikTok hobby and how it was distracting me while I was going through my legal nightmare. I asked her if she thought I had narcissistic traits. I wanted to understand myself because I didn't feel like a nice person. There were times I'd manipulated situations to get the best out of people. Also because I hated injustice with a passion. I responded to it with anger and frustration which sometimes spilled out onto those closest to me.

She told me that personality disorders like the more extreme forms of narcissism are pretty much untreatable and do not harm the person they affect; they harm others. So no, it was highly unlikely. In her opinion I had ADHD, a past eating disorder and was possibly suffering from PTSD which I already knew.

Also, I was having a hard time accepting that the people we thought were our friends wanted nothing to do with us. I thought we were liked at work, but none of our staff called to ask how we were doing. I'd suffered break ups and rejection in the past, but this was on another level.

I spent days questioning my actions. All my life I have grafted in business. I've never been afraid to roll up my sleeves and put in the hours that were needed to be successful. Money was never the goal; it was always about the challenge and proving everyone wrong. I just wanted my business or product to be the best.

I tried my hand as an estate agent after giving birth to my only child Molly because I struggled with being a full-time mother. I felt guilty at not being fulfilled by looking after my baby. But my brain craved a bigger challenge. So I committed to working Saturdays and Sundays and loved it. It was my first experience in sales and I thrived.

My colleagues watched with envy as I steadily outpaced them on performance. I sold the most houses, often exceeding the targets the company set. Clients would send letters telling my superiors what an asset I was and that they'd recommend me to their friends. My customer conversion rate was near 100%. It frustrated the competitors who often tried to poach me.

Selling houses didn't feel like work. I loved every day of it and shamefully I admit, I probably loved it more than being a mother to Molly. Recognising how I valued work over motherhood has been a tough reality to absorb.

CAPITAL PUNISHMENT

The first business I started was a wedding planning company. I knew it would be difficult for people in Lincolnshire to afford luxury weddings, unlike in London where there's wealth in abundance. It had become something of a statement to have someone remove the stress of budgeting and planning the day and planners were charging thousands.

To make that work in Lincolnshire I had to make it affordable. Back then on average people spent between £5,000 and £12,000 on their big day. As their money would only stretch so far, I made them focus on their priorities, whether it be the venue, dress or honeymoon. I only charged an affordable fee of £250, confident that from an average of six home visits I could make their day amazing.

I had planned to arrange five weddings in my first year. By the end, I'd organised 46! I visited all the venues and bridal shops and inspected the cars. Then I asked the suppliers for 10% for bringing them new business. Now I had two incomes.

It was the beginning of the internet and everyone was lost, floating around in the ether. So I bought a domain name, paid a web designer to create a homepage and charged other wedding related businesses to link their websites to mine. Now I had three incomes!

Where did I fail? The paperwork bamboozled me. I could arrange complex weddings, but accounts and invoices weren't my strong point. Plus, I wasn't good at asking for money. I had no idea I had ADHD back then. I would probably have been far more successful if I had.

CHAPTER 12

TikTok Gives Me a Business Idea

Financially we were in trouble. I had to make an income. I knew my mental health was too fragile to cope with any kind of conventional job, so I went back to my inventing days. I often told others that if you want to create something make a note any time you are frustrated by a product or come across a situation that bothers you. Then devise a solution to make the process faster and easier. This was how I came up with my Magnamole cable threading tool.

Within half an hour of watching TikTok I could see a new venture: a TV show. I contacted a legal expert from my "Dragons' Den" days to draw up a contract to protect my idea. I'd devised a unique competition based on the fact that TikTok is toxic in many ways and the winner would be the content creator who exemplified all that is good about the platform.

I believed if I could get my TV show off the ground, I could make some instant money and also generate some publicity for my book about our Buildadeck ordeal. I was excited about both opportunities.

During the lockdowns a few creators had made it big and were now living millionaire lifestyles. They would dance or sing or perform a comedy routine. But the new generation of TikTok participants had got it all wrong. They were begging for gifts, creating explosive arguments and publicly humiliating themselves and others for views.

What I noticed with all of them was that they all seem to have survived some kind of terrible event. As a result, some had become narcissistic and some had gone the opposite way and become empaths. Everyone develops their own particular coping mechanism to childhood trauma that stays with them for life.

I recalled from my Magnamole days that inventors also suffer from being exploited, having met many of them at various shows. Half of their brain is wired to problem solve, but most don't have the determination, tenacity, social skills or ability to take their product to market. Some of the greatest ideas have been created by trusting people who have then had their inventions stolen. I've seen private equity companies destroy them, leaving them disillusioned and depressed.

For example, one of my dear friends, Kane Kramner was the original inventor of the digital iPlayer. He fought so hard to protect his invention that he lost his sanity. In the end his concept was taken from him and others went on to make billions. The theft of intellectual property has made a lot of individuals very rich. Look at Bill Gates and Mark Zuckerberg.

I contacted my lawyer friend to see how I could protect my TV show idea. He said to detail as much as I could and then write to some agencies. After I'd done all the necessary paperwork, I reached out to Matt Arnold from GMTV to see what he thought of my idea. He was an enthusiastic character like me and passed my concept on to a production company. They loved it.

CAPITAL PUNISHMENT

We discussed the venue where the show would be filmed and what kind of TikTok creators would be the contestants. Everything was going full steam ahead, but then out of the blue the production company pulled out. They said it was too similar to another show, even though there was nothing else like it.

I contacted another company and they invited me to their studios. They said they could help fund the cameras and the crew through a ventures firm and in return I would receive a third of the revenue. A couple of weeks later they stopped taking my calls and didn't answer my messages.

Mindful of the balance between persevering and being a nuisance, I reached out to other TV production companies and anyone I knew who could help get my idea off the ground. My hopes had been raised with all the positive feedback, so I was troubled that I was now being stonewalled.

I emailed the producers to ask why they'd changed their minds but they didn't reply. Then I was introduced to another guy called Paul. He was a good friend of a person called Gerry who used to hang out with my brother when we were young and we'd kept in touch over the years. This Paul seemed to come along at just the right time.

CAPITAL PUNISHMENT

CHAPTER 13

SAS Paul and the Production Companies

Paul was an ex-SAS commander who was often interviewed on world events. He was friendly and charismatic and made John and I both feel at ease. He told us about the TV shows he had in the pipeline and revealed that he too had ADHD and dyslexia. He said it was a sign of intelligence and many people in NASA had the same neuro divergent issues.

When we told him about Elina and the Buildadeck situation he agreed that it appeared to be a deliberate ploy to build up our hopes before we were hit with the shock of having the equity in our house frozen.

We spent hours with him discussing our ordeal with Commercide and Nick and he also agreed that our story needed to be told. Then he asked if we had considered the possibility that the fake home buyer Elina may have planted listening devices in our house and told us we should have it swept for bugs. Finally, I told him about my TV show idea and my attempts to sell the idea.

The previous month, after picking myself back up off the floor from the shock of the freezing order, I had flown to the US with a view to speaking to Netflix about making a documentary about our ordeal with Commercide. "If you don't ask, you don't get" has always been my motto.

CAPITAL PUNISHMENT

My neighbour was going to a horse owner's exhibition in Texas and suggested I tag along on her trip. Instead of flying straight home, we could drive along Route 66. The trip took seven days and we stopped at many interesting locations along the way.

Finally, we arrived in LA. I naively believed I could just turn up at Netflix's offices and ask for a meeting with someone to discuss my ideas. I'd taken a copy of the book I had already written to prove I could achieve success, so I was confident they would take me seriously.

To my disappointment the visit was a waste of time. I was greeted at the gates by two armed guards who asked for proof of an appointment. Nobody could access the building unless they had a pre-arranged meeting. They even refused to pass on the letter I'd written or give anyone my book. One of the guards told me to go around the corner to the post office and mail it to them from there. So that's what I did.

I felt quite deflated but I was glad I went. The trip was amazing and we got to see LA's beautiful houses before the wildfires destroyed them at the beginning of 2025.

To my great delight, Paul loved my idea and introduced me to a documentary producer called Natalie. I sent her an email asking her to sign a non-disclosure agreement (NDA) before I told her about the show's format. My lawyer friend Steve strongly advised me not to reveal anything to anyone in the media without it, because plagiarism was rife in that industry.

To my surprise, Natalie responded shortly afterwards saying her lawyers advised her against signing NDAs, but she respected that I wanted to protect my TV show concept. She explained that her company was already committed to other projects for the foreseeable future and wished me well.

Paul's efforts to spread the word about making a Buildadeck documentary resulted in interest from someone who wanted to do a podcast about my success on "Dragons' Den." but even nothing came of that.

When I have a burning idea like I had with my winning invention, I'll work at speed around the clock, so I had to learn to be patient, which is something I'm not good at. I was discovering that 99% of people never do what they say they will do. My frustration was building.

I had kept in touch with a good friend of mine from school called Marcus who also knew my friend Gerry. (More about him later.) Marcus had a wicked sense of humour and constantly made people laugh. I needed to inject some fun into the TV show and it struck me that he would be the perfect person to partner with.

After he'd signed the NDA, Marcus, his wife, John and I sat down around the table and I presented my task-based contest for social media content makers. Marcus thought it was great and we continued to meet regularly to discuss the idea. I also gave him a considerable number of shares.

Over dinner one evening, Marcus randomly mentioned to John and myself that he had joined the Freemasons. It was a little out of the blue, but because of his chequered past, nothing surprised me. He said he'd had to dress up in a cloak, wear a hat and hold a sword and repeat a pledge. As part of the initiation ceremony, he also had to wait in a cupboard, then knock on the door of the meeting hall several times and ask to enter. The way he described everything had us all in fits of laughter.

I gave Marcus my notes for the TV show and he said he'd put them into a more structured format. He came to the house a few times. Then he went radio silent.

I called and sent texts. Usually, he would respond within a day. Something had changed. I was frustrated because he hadn't been in contact for so long, so I sent him a message that was intended to be tongue in cheek saying, "Please tell me you haven't gone somewhere else with this idea."

After a couple of days he responded, saying he'd been very ill with a fever and had hoped I would have had more respect than to suggest that he would betray me. I felt awful that I'd upset him. This is part of my problem. I speak my mind and later have to apologise because I'm a people pleaser. But in this case, I was right to have my suspicions about him.

I received another email from Natalie. She wanted me to arrange a conference call with her and a colleague. After what Paul had said about her stealing other people's ideas I didn't dare reply. All the waiting as well as all the raised hopes and disappointments were starting to get me down.

I didn't know if it was my imagination or if I was being gaslit. It felt like I was going round in circles. By now we had shared the TV show idea and our private equity company nightmare with lots of people, but for some reason it never got further than a couple of meetings.

Perhaps symbolically, it was around this time a pigeon flew into one of the large glass windows at the front of our house. There was a loud thud, then it dropped to the ground and sat there with a broken wing, still alive, looking at me desperately. I was sure it would pass away to another world very soon and left it there to die.

To my surprise it was still alive and lying there in the same position the next day. I felt terrible for leaving it to suffer and carefully placed it in a cage with some water and food and called the RSPCA. Nobody came.

I watched it for days as it hopped out of the cage and went outside onto the grass where it was vulnerable to attack. I cried for that pigeon because it represented what I was going through. I felt its desperation as it hoped for death and saw how it instinctively struggled to survive despite being broken and fearful that a predator would take it.

When you promise your loved ones that you will never attempt to take your life again it forces you to survive despite everything being against you. I've often hated living in my head and longed to escape, but that promise to my family meant more. Ultimately, I'm thankful for it because it has meant I'm still here today.

SAS Paul had introduced us to another production company who was interested in the TV show. They also had access to ITN and the investigative news series "Dispatches" so I asked Paul to follow up with them.

He confirmed that they wanted to meet me. But the week we agreed to get together they had to report on the Jay Slater case in Tenerife. I sent Paul a text asking if someone had contacted ITN to put them off covering our story. It had been four months of thinking we were getting somewhere, waiting for the next step to happen and then getting nothing but silence.

Paul told me to speak with Natalie again. After everything he'd said about her I was starting to lose interest with my TV show idea and the documentary. I was beginning to think everyone was raising my hopes and then deliberately dashing them as part of some game or warped conspiracy to chip away at my sanity.

CHAPTER 14

Tiffany Cianci

In September 2024, when I was scrolling through TikTok, I came across a live interview with Robert F Kennedy Jr and a young woman called Tiffany Cianci. The split screen showed several people waiting to ask Kennedy questions. At the time he was running for president of the United States and had just written "The Real Anthony Fauci."

His understanding of the real-life struggles for the average citizen caught my interest. He said that because of this, he'd been cancelled by the mainstream news channels and banned on almost all social media platforms. The left-wing globalists hate him because he doesn't fall into line with their agenda, which is to protect the interests of the big corporations and the billionaire super-elite; the 1% of the 1%.

Sadly, the public's perception of him has been manipulated to make him appear as something of an anti-vax, anti-establishment crackpot. I have never really had much faith in any of our governments because corruption is not unique to any of them. By contrast this man seemed to have a moral compass.

He was talking about how he'd make small businesses a priority and was outraged by the harassment Tiffany had been subjected to by a large private equity firm and was personally advising her in her quest for justice. When he'd finished answering questions, he left the live chat while Tiffany continued.

I don't know what possessed me, but I requested to join the conversation and she accepted. I told her how I'd suffered at the hands of predatory equity firms on two occasions The latest had fabricated a legal case against me, put a freezing order on the sale of my house which had traumatised me so much I'd tried to take my life. After the group video chat ended Tiffany said she wanted to talk to me privately the following day.

I did some research on Tiffany and discovered that she is a prominent speaker on regulating the private equity capital investment sector. Tiffany and her lawyer are fighting against a billion-dollar investment firm and their army of attorneys due to the terror tactics they subjected her to when she was the owner of a Little Gym franchise in Maryland, USA. It's a David and Goliath battle, just like the one John and I are going through.

The next day we connected via Zoom and Tiffany explained that she'd run her franchise business since 2017, but like all the other owners was forced to close for over a year due to the Covid mandates. Due to a dramatic loss of income, the owner of the entire operation decided to sell out to a large investment firm.

The private equity company was originally presented as a "marketing partner," but it soon became clear that all they wanted was money. The firm demanded that all the franchisees sign an agreement allowing fees and royalty payments to be deducted from their bank accounts. Tiffany refused to sign because there wasn't a lot of extra revenue to be squeezed out of the business. She organised a union in an attempt to negotiate with their new "investors."

CAPITAL PUNISHMENT

The equity firm decided to make an example out of her in order to terrorise everyone else into compliance. They terminated her franchise for non-payment of fees. She had been sending them checks, but they had deliberately not cashed them. Then they demanded she pay them a termination penalty payment of £100,000.

They also sent letters to all of the members of the Franchise Association saying she had abused children, stolen money and owed them tens of thousands of dollars. (None of this was true, and they were later found guilty of defamation.)

This private equity firm also hired private investigators and paid a $120,000 bribe to her landlord to not renew her lease. They also paid people to stalk her and her family and commissioned a felon to forge documents as "evidence" in support of their case.

She told me private equity firms are stealing whatever they can from franchise owners all over the country. Every day small businesses with no way of defending themselves against these billion-dollar investment firms are being ruined.

This is because basically all private equity companies do is destroy. But as they destroy, they create money which is funnelled into the bank accounts of a few multi-billionaires. Meanwhile, the once healthy business is left bankrupt and empty. They are like vampires, sucking the life out of communities, corporations and workforces. The scary thing is, these predators have now infiltrated almost every facet of modern life in their endless search for profits.

Then she told me something so shocking I could hardly believe it. At the time Tiffany was going through her fight with these investors she'd been pregnant. Unfortunately, she'd had a fall in the shower which meant it was a high-risk pregnancy. When she was at the hospital, the equity firm's lawyers somehow found out about her situation and decided to exploit it.

While she was on bed rest, they repeatedly issued subpoenas which required her to go to court in another state five hours' drive away. She even received emails saying if she didn't attend, she'd be arrested and put in jail.

Because her pregnancy complications inconvenienced the efficacy of their lawfare, the equity firm then filed a motion to compel her to have an abortion. (In arbitration you don't have to follow the law, whereas in a normal court they wouldn't have been allowed to apply that kind of pressure.) Her counsel received an email demanding her pregnancy was terminated by 7:00pm the next day. Moreover, if she didn't, she'd be penalised!

Ultimately, the stress of the litigation coupled with her high-risk pregnancy resulted in the baby being stillborn. In addition, Tiffany and her family have nearly lost their house dealing with the constant influx of litigation. She said the only person that has tried to help her was Robert F Kennedy Jr who'd read about her in the news. You can see her compelling interview with him on "American Stories with RFK Jr" on his YouTube channel.

Hearing about her struggles helped put my own into perspective. It was somewhat reassuring to know that John and I had not been taken advantage of because of some fault of ours. The equity firms' "jump scare" manoeuvres are well known in the industry.

Tiffany now dedicates her time exposing their cruel and mercenary game and defending "the little guy" by testifying before the Federal Trade Commission and Congress. She is a strong, extremely knowledgeable and eloquent woman who has maintained her fighting spirit despite a constant onslaught of litigation and financial hardship. She has my total respect.

I called my ex-SAS friend Paul to update him about my discussions with Tiffany. He told me, "Great! It's meat on the bones." Then he asked me to email him a list of bullet points to summarise our conversation and said a producer at ITN was going to take my story to his commissioner and get us a slot on Channel 4 or ITN.

Of course, I heard nothing more.

CAPITAL PUNISHMENT

CHAPTER 15

Private Equity Capital is Money from Hell

I found two other companies in the UK who appeared to have suffered similar fates to ours. It looked like the directors had been forced out for some fake infringement and replaced by the equity company's own personnel. In one of them, Commercide's directors had taken over as owners just like they had at Buildadeck.

I tried to contact the original directors. One seemed to have vanished off the face of the earth. I hoped he hadn't tried to kill himself. The other lived in Bath. He ran a health food business and Commercide had appointed their own directors with Nick becoming the majority shareholder the day the owner retired.

I drove over to see him but he wasn't home, so I left a message with a man who was looking after his house while he was away in Portugal. He returned my call later that day. I asked if he'd been wrongly accused of theft. He said he hadn't but he wanted to speak to me when he got back to the UK. For legal reasons he didn't tell me much except that his opinion of one of his company's new directors was the same as ours; he was a piece of work.

Then a friend of mine in the US did some research and sent me a copy of a study from Stanford Law. It spelt out all the devious ways business owners are being ousted from their companies and being tied up in complex legalities. When I received it, I cried. Seeing that their evil methods were well known, yet they were still getting away with it was too much to bear. I would like to add here that I cannot believe all private equity companies are corrupt. Some of them must operate with a degree of concern for the companies they take over.

I also found a study written by Lord Prem Sikka of The House of Lords who also viewed these private equity companies as dangerous opportunists. He demanded that regulations were introduced to prevent these firms from inventing sham complaints and launching smear campaigns to weaponise the legal system in order to oust business's owners and sell their companies on at a profit.

Tiffany Ciani explained to me why private equity is now the preferred investment mechanism of the ultra-wealthy. 20 years ago, they would have had to hold an investment for 10 years for the tax benefits (where profits are taxed as capital gains or investment returns, not income). This meant they had a goal of long-term success. Now they can hold something for as little as a year and flip it to the next guy allowing them to benefit much faster with little liability.

They don't have any interest in the success of the companies they acquire. They just strip mine them by aggressively reducing costs and selling off assets and flip them repeatedly. It's looting justified by solid investment returns.

A private equity firm pools cash from investors and uses those funds, along with money borrowed from other sources to take over a target company. Having acquired its target, it may decimate the workforce, fire the management team, install new executives or move it offshore. It can also liquidate the company's assets to pay back investors and line their own pockets before selling it on; a tactic known as a "buy, strip and flip."

As the vice president of one equity firm owner admits, "You can't have a trace of sentimentality. You have to be able to slash and burn. How do I live with myself? In a big house in the suburbs, with my wife and kids."

Recessions and or times of economic stress like Covid are major feeding frenzies for these predatory firms. They can pick up businesses on the cheap and then integrate them within a larger umbrella corporation. This has resulted in a massive transfer of money upwards to the wealth-obsessed so-called global elite.

During Covid there was a big meeting of media and tech moguls, CEOs, and other high-ranking officials in Sun Valley ("summer camp for billionaires") in Idaho. They were struck by a survey that showed very few people trusted the corporations, but a huge percentage trusted and supported the independent retailer, especially individual and family-owned businesses. So, they decided they needed to invest in small businesses while keeping them looking small.

They let these companies keep their original names and identities so the public still thinks they are independently owned. (They don't suspect anything until they go online and notice their website looks generic or try to speak to someone and get put through to a call centre in India.)

In addition, these billionaires knew it would be preferential to choose companies people are emotionally tied to. These are the businesses offering products and services that people pay for, no matter the cost and will even take out loans for them. Companies like veterinary centres, fertility centres, nursing care facilities, children's daycare and funeral homes attracted guaranteed business.

Private equity companies like The Blackstone Group (the former parent company of Blackrock) now own our land, our grocery stores, waste collection services, loan companies and our law firms. You name it, they've bought it. Now they basically have control over all aspects of our lives and their grip is getting tighter by the day.

The wealth of these massive corporations allows them to influence politicians and push through regulations that make it easier for them and harder for any remaining small independent business in that market sector. They have rigged the system so that it's almost impossible for small businesses to survive. And that's the point. With the absence of any competition, prices are hiked to whatever the company at the top of the pyramid dictates.

Our houses will be the next thing they acquire by stealth. They will force us into debt by pushing financing and raising interest rates until we will have no choice but to hand them over. The globalists are right. The way it's all set up inevitably we will end up owning nothing, but we will be far from happy.

All our rights have been taken away from us. Legal aid has gone and Citizens Advice is the next service to be made redundant. Independent business owners are all alone fighting for survival while the money lenders smile, knowing our fate is in their hands.

Knowing this bigger picture, I have shifted my perspective and almost see it as something of an honour that John and I have been targeted for destruction. I now have a powerful and important purpose. If it means spending the rest of my life screaming out to make people aware of what's going on.

Although it's human nature to side with the rich, powerful wrongdoer rather than the weaker, poorer truth teller I still have hope. My belief in the power of God and all that exists in the spiritual world makes me think that one day "the meek shall inherit the earth."

CAPITAL PUNISHMENT

CHAPTER 16

The Police Don't See a Crime

Knowing what I do about the way private equity firms operate behind the scenes, hiring people to stalk you, lying about you, sending private investigators to delve into your personal life and bribing people to help break you down, I now see why such a strange assortment of people have entered our lives these past few years.

I believe Elina's job was to raise my hopes that I'd sell my house because she appeared just a week before Buildadeck went to court to put a freezing order on any future house sale. The idea was to leave me shattered. But Elina messed up when she borrowed money from me and couldn't afford to pay it back. It was my chance to find out more about her.

At around 4:00am one morning she called me to say she was stuck in Manchester and needed the money to get home. So, I got John to transfer £500 to her account. A day or two later she asked to borrow another £1500, which I declined.

I spoke to a few retired officers who'd left the force and asked if she had committed a crime. One ex-police officer told me her tactics were similar to people who use love bombing to get what they want by deception and yes, that was illegal, so I reported her to the police.

CAPITAL PUNISHMENT

The officer spent a lot of the time writing down my statement. Then a few days later I received a call saying that because I lived in Scunthorpe and Elina lived in Hull my complaint had to be handled over there. The case was sent to a police constable in Hull who I had to constantly email to prompt some action. He promised multiple times to speak to me but never did. Yet more frustration!

After six months I still hadn't been able to speak to him on the phone, so I contacted the original police officer in Scunthorpe and told her I was being stone walled and asked how I could escalate the investigation. My concerns were relayed back to the officer in Hull.

This went on for months. I'd receive the odd email saying he was unable to speak to Elina but promised to have a response within a couple of weeks. Then he informed me that Elina had offered to return the £500 I'd lent her and he needed my bank details so she could do the transfer.

Until Elina explained who had sent her and what the purpose of the house buying pretence was, I wasn't interested in getting my money back or giving him my bank details. I needed confirmation that she was part of some kind of scheme to mess with my mind.

I checked to see if there had been any Euro Lottery winners in Lithuania. As far as I could see there were none. In fact, there had never been a winner in that country. Elina's social media platforms confirmed that she did have an uncle in the USA.

Of course, after I reported her to the police Elina conveniently lost her phone. I believe this was to dispose of any evidence connecting her to America and

Commercide. She left me several voicemails that were also passed on to the police. She sounded drunk and desperate and said she was so sorry for what she'd done and insisted her decision not to buy my house was due to nothing more than a change of mind.

All the messages she left were jumbled and made no sense, but she did mention she was still trying to go to America to see her uncle who had suddenly had a bad stroke but his wife wouldn't allow her or her mother to visit.

After this I gave her several chances to return the money she'd borrowed but as usual, every time we arranged to meet, she came up with some bullshit excuse. She'd say she was coming to my house then cancel and promise to come the following day. I offered to collect the money myself, but of course there was another reason why I couldn't.

People ask why I lent her money in the first place. I knew I couldn't ask the police to investigate someone for changing their mind about buying a house. I knew she had been sent to build up my hopes so they could be crushed. When she had called asking to borrow money it was an opportunity to get her to expose her part in the equity firm's gameplan once and for all.

As the police had taken no action, I had no choice but to lodge a complaint against the policeman in Hull. To do this, you have to call a special number and state your grievance on a recorded line within a set time limit. Nobody listened my message because when the police called me back, I had to explain everything again.

Fortunately, the person handling my call was very patient and agreed that the case needed investigating. I was informed that because I'd filed a complaint against the officer in Hull he would no longer be handling my case or contacting me again.

So, you can imagine my shock when two days later I received a call from the same police officer in Hull from a withheld number! He said he would bring Elina's money to me himself and the transaction would be recorded as evidence on his body camera.

"No! I've raised a complaint against you. I was told you wouldn't contact me so please don't call me again," I insisted, annoyed that they couldn't even get this right.

"I'm not aware of any complaint. I'm bringing you the money because the case against Elina needs to be closed," he replied flatly.

"No!" I protested, "I am not interested in getting any money back until the whole situation is investigated properly and until you find out who sent her to my house." How many times did I have to repeat myself? I'd sent this policeman many emails telling him why this was the most important aspect of the case, but he obviously didn't have the time or inclination to look into it.

"I'm sorry. I don't see that any crime has been committed and neither does my superior. Basically, there's nothing to investigate," he informed me.

After this, every time I called the station I was transferred to an answer machine of a male traffic police officer. I constantly asked why nothing was being done. Finally, I was told in their opinion, no offence had taken place.

I still fail to see how producing fraudulent bank statements showing millions of pounds, befriending me under the pretence of buying my house and then borrowing money she had no intention of repaying was not a crime.

CAPITAL PUNISHMENT

CHAPTER 17

Our Visit from a Freemason

Out of the blue I received a message from a guy on TikTok called Paul – yes, another Paul – who said he wanted to speak to me privately. He said he was an "earth angel" and spiritual healer who helped people along their lifetime's journey. He told me his activities were being watched on social media and he had to be careful.

We talked for a while and I told him all about the situation I was in with Commercide Ventures and how I needed to get my story out. He asked what kind of audience I wanted to reach and I told him ideally it was people in the United States and Canada. I explained that I was writing a book which covered everything in detail and needed to find others who had also suffered at the hands of this particular investment firm.

Paul told me he also had an active channel on YouTube and could possibly arrange an interview with a director friend of his called Paul Donnellon (Paul again!). He said he had recently started dating a lady called Pauline (this is getting ridiculous now) and they were going to stay at a lodge park just outside of Scunthorpe. Pauline wanted to visit her sister who lived nearby, during which time he could meet me sometime that weekend.

Gullible me suspecting nothing untoward was optimistic that this guy could help. Little did I know that another round of crazy-making weirdness was about to commence. I told John about my new TikTok friend and he was sceptical. I convinced him that this guy might be able to help us, so he agreed to let him visit.

One of the many lessons I was to learn was that my craving for validation meant I often trusted the wrong people. John had noticed I did this and thought it was endearing, but he questioned why my self-esteem was so low that I constantly needed to be acknowledged. Most of the time I was trying to impress people who could not give a damn.

Unfortunately, because of my insatiable need to be heard, I ended up giving too much information to this Paul, going into depth about talking to Tiffany Cianci and Robert F Kennedy Jr and telling him ITN was doing a documentary. I also told him about Elina and how she'd pretended she was interested in buying our house and had kept her act going for months.

On August 3rd 2024, Paul and his girlfriend arrived early in the morning. The minute they came through the door Paul told us he'd left his car in Scunthorpe because it had a flat tire. The plan was that Pauline would drop him off at the garage in a few hours' time and he would return when she went to visit her sister. It wasn't until later that John and I questioned why they had travelled in two separate cars.

Paul and his girlfriend were very impressed by the house, so we gave them a guided tour. As we stood in the bedroom looking out onto the river Paul asked if we had ever wondered if Elina's motive in pretending to be a buyer was so she could plant listening devices. This possibility had crossed our minds and we'd told the police about our suspicions.

CAPITAL PUNISHMENT

I was only just beginning to investigate the spiritual side of things and had bought John and myself bracelets with stones that are supposed to protect you from evil. Within the first few minutes of sitting down to eat brunch Paul asked what the bracelets were for. When I told him, he asked us to remove them immediately because they were bad omens. He also said we should have our house blessed and knew someone in Scunthorpe who could do it.

I replied that my friend Rita was a spiritual person and had already cleansed the house with sage. I wasn't a believer or a disbeliever, but any help to rid curses or bad energy from our environment was welcome at this point.

Pauline then asked which school I'd gone to and to my surprise she said she'd been to the same one. Being a couple of years older than me I presumed my brother would know her. Then she asked me where I'd grown up. So, I told her I'd lived at Whitfield Road since I was born until the age of 13. Bizarrely she told me her first husband had lived on the same street.

Intrigued, I dug a little deeper because I knew every kid around that area. She said he had lived in one of the bungalows. This confused me because I didn't recognise his name and was sure that no children lived in any of those properties. (The day afterwards I checked with my brother and my friends and they all said Pauline had never gone to my school.)

Seeing my doubtful expression, Pauline changed the subject and told us how she'd met Paul. (Incidentally, throughout our conversations Paul kept calling Pauline "Sharon." Both John and I were a little disturbed by this. It must have happened at least half a dozen times and we both mentioned it after they left.)

Paul didn't talk much about spiritual healing, probably because John had said he didn't believe in any of that mumbo jumbo, but knew it comforted me so he went along with it. But Paul did explain how his spiritual journey as a healer began.

He told us his ex-wife in Ireland had children of her own and he'd had some conflict with them. Also, before they split up, she'd racked up tens of thousands of pounds of debt which finally broke their marriage. So, he flew back to the UK and was now working as a plumber and lived in Cardiff, but was heading down to London the following week. Apparently, he'd discovered his spiritual abilities on his own healing journey and knew he could help others.

It was time for Pauline to visit her sister in Scunthorpe so they both went off to collect Paul's car. He returned on his own 40 minutes later. The minute he entered the house his demeanour switched. He seemed to be on some kind of mission.

The first thing he did was to ask if he could charge his phone because the battery was low. He went straight over to John's laptop and plugged an extension lead into it. In hindsight, he could have possibly downloaded everything from the device, but of course we have no proof that this is what happened. We suspected nothing at the time and only thought about it when things turned scary.

Paul wasted no time in telling us he used to be a Freemason. He informed us that four people run the world and that everyone believes there are 33 levels of Freemasonry, but in fact there are 42. He then produced a little black book with all my details in it and started asking questions about the things I'd told him.

He wanted to know what I hoped to achieve by writing a book and how many copies of my last book I'd sold. Then he enquired about the companies that had hired me as an after-dinner speaker. I gave him a few names, but his questions unsettled me.

He said he had watched my "Dragons' Den" episode and could see I was an intelligent woman and should use my creative skills to do something productive. I said I'd thought about doing something to link AI to the NHS and the police force because these public services were so overwhelmed they were unable to function properly. Since the lockdowns, doctors' surgeries, hospitals, dentists and the police had struggled to meet public demand.

Paul then looked at me and said that I was the problem. The book I was writing was also a problem and that I was playing with fire. To prove the seriousness of what he was saying he told me to do a search on Commercide's CEO and I would see that he's a member of the Illuminati. He was right. I took a screenshot of the details just in case he amended his status.

Then he told us he knew an SAS commander who'd been sent to assassinate president Mugabe, but the operation had to be aborted. After this he said the Royal Ulster Constabulary were targeting people but kept getting it wrong. Another story he relayed to us was how he had met with an Asian doctor in London who was one of the four world leaders and wore an emerald ring. He said the top tier Level 42 Masons run the government, our legal system, all the banks and ultimately the entire world.

I thought, "Is this guy for real?" Then his stories became more serious and shocking. He told us the planes that crashed into the Twin Towers on 9/11 were remote controlled and the entire attack had been planned by the CIA. The passengers on the original plane had been flown elsewhere and disposed of.

The next thing he mentioned was that he knew that a bomb had been planted in a ride at Euro Disney while it was closed for maintenance. I suspect he wanted me to go to the authorities with all this information so I'd look crazy. I did actually tell the police, but they didn't even take a statement.

Then he went on to say both good and bad people go to heaven, that the Royal family are part of the Masonic elite and Robert F Kennedy Jr was at the upper end of the powerful globalist cabal who supported Israel and the goals of the World Economic Forum.

He warned me that if I spoke out about any of this, mine and John's lives would be at risk. To my horror he then informed me that I should have died at Christmas and "they" could snipe me from two miles away if they wanted. He said all this while looking through our large glass windows and pointing to the river. Apparently, I had become a big problem when I'd spoken to Tiffany and Kennedy.

He asked us what we thought about our fake prospective house buyer Elina. I told him that I suspected her uncle in America had possibly borrowed money from the predators and couldn't afford to pay it back. She had mentioned that her uncle had suffered a very bad stroke and she'd been trying to get some money together to visit him. She'd left me numerous drunk voicemails asking me to help her find out which hospital he was in as his wife would not tell her.

At this point I noticed that Paul was looking at his watch. By now he'd positioned himself at the dining room table with the large picture windows behind him. While he'd been talking, a car had driven up the road to our house, stopped, waited and then turned around in the driveway before heading off.

"Have you noticed you're being watched," he remarked casually.

Then he weirdly asked if I was aware that my daughter was depressed. I said no to both of these questions which sent shivers down my spine. Now I just wanted him to leave. So, I stood up and said John and I were meeting friends later that evening and we needed to get ready. He knew he'd spooked me.

"When did you last contact your business partner Paul?" he asked as he got up to leave. Only he didn't call him Paul. He referred to him by his nickname "Yorkie" which neither myself or John had mentioned once. Without saying anything to each other, both John and I instantly knew he had been sent by someone with connections to Commercide.

I told him the last time I'd spoken to him was just after Christmas and that if Commercide was relying on him to lie in court, Paul had made it very clear that he wouldn't do that. While Paul had chosen Commercide over us to protect his family, for the same reasons he would not risk going to prison for perjury.

Then he changed tack and said I wasn't a big enough threat and "they" weren't even that bothered about the house because it was only worth a couple of million. He asked how we'd been able to keep it this long. Presumably he had to report back on our financial situation and how desperate we were to sell. We told him we had limited savings but were okay for now.

"Listen, I know you are both hard working and straight and to be honest you should never have been targeted. I've been sent here to negotiate. What is it that you guys want?" he asked, to our total amazement.

Omg! This was what I'd been hoping to hear for months!

"I want a public apology from Nick for accusing us of being thieves," I answered, "We also want our legal fees reimbursed. As far my shares go, I don't care. They can have them. Money only seems to go to people who are ruthless and that's not me."

"It's impossible to get a public apology because it doesn't work like that," Paul replied, "But the good news is I know your money will be returned but not directly into your bank account. It'll be in a less obvious way."

John and I looked at each other in disbelief.

As he was leaving Paul said ominously, "You know I could go to the States and take out the CEO of Commercide but it would cost you guys a lot of money and would probably take too long. But as I said, all your legal problems are going away. It's just going to take some time, so hang in there!"

Finally, he said, "I have something for you," and went to his car. He returned holding a candle and a blue crystal.

"I want you to go into a dark room together and light this candle while you both manifest your desired outcome. Stay there until the candle is completely burned away."

After he'd gone John and I looked at each other. I put my finger to my lips and pointed to the ceiling. He was thinking the same thing as me. We headed up to the balcony where we always went when we wanted to talk without being recorded.

"It's real! He really is from the Masons!" John exclaimed.

We laughed with relief, recalling how he'd said "they" had got us wrong and had made a mistake. Now they were asking us what we wanted! Surely this meant they'd be offering us a settlement. It was the least they could do, because realistically they owed us damages for everything they'd put us through.

All I could say was, "Oh my god. Is this really happening? It's like a film!

We were elated that our nightmare might finally be ending. We would get to live our lives again, only this time we'd appreciate them so much more. That night for the first time in forever I slept soundly and woke up feeling lighter. The weight of worry was gone.

CAPITAL PUNISHMENT

CHAPTER 18

Reality Sets In

That evening we went over to our friends' house and told them everything that had happened. They sat with their mouths open in disbelief as we relayed everything Paul had said. I had never felt such relief in my life. Even having experienced all the amazing, heart stopping high points like winning "The British Inventor's Show," "Dragon's Den" and "Business Woman of The Year," this was far better. This was the best feeling of all.

We had lived with shame and anger for so long, feeling hopeless and helpless. When you have done nothing but sit in desperation for over a year, to suddenly feel free of that burden was magical. This had to be one of the best nights of my life. We all celebrated with a few drinks and toasted to better days ahead.

The next morning, I woke in the early hours with a gut-wrenching feeling. Terror gripped me harder than before. Things didn't add up. I replayed all of Paul's conversations from the previous day and was struck with huge dread.

Our house is made nearly all from glass. It's a contemporary building on top of a hill overlooking a river and is surrounded by fields and a couple of roads. We were sitting ducks! If Paul could take out the CEO of Commercide then why not us? I began to shake. I woke John up and told him my fears.

CAPITAL PUNISHMENT

When Paul had first arrived with his "girlfriend" they had seemed lovely. But later, when we were waiting for him to leave, I was struck with a horrible feeling

of foreboding. My sixth sense has never been wrong. Their couple act was all bullshit. I suspected Paul was a Freemason and had been sent by Commercide. I did some research and was shocked to discover that he'd only started his TikTok platform a couple of days after me.

I started to question everything like a detective while John listened intently. Why had they travelled in two cars? Why did another car turn up outside our house and park there as if they were watching us? Why was Paul constantly checking his phone?

Why was the logo on Paul's TikTok page a handgun and a dove? Why did he think my daughter Molly was depressed? I'd never even mentioned her name. Was my family now at risk? How did Paul know my ex-business partner's nickname? It was very unusual and nothing like his real name. You would only know these things if you had been briefed by someone close to us.

Why did he say I should have died at Christmas? Why did he want to know how many books I'd sold previously? Why did he say I was risking my life if I spoke out? Why was the candle in a plastic container? Was it carcinogenic or laced with chemicals? Everyone knows you only get candles in glass, metal or ceramic containers.

When he was charging his phone had he copied all the files on John's laptop to see what evidence we had before full disclosure? If he really was a spiritual healer why on earth would he talk about taking people out?

Was the world I had always believed to have existed, with its civil laws and social rules just one huge lie? Did something happen to Elina's uncle in America? Were all the conspiracy theories you see on social media real?

My mind was now driving me crazy. Who could I trust? Were we safe? Would anyone believe what was happening to us? Would anyone believe the conversation we'd just had with this Freemason?

Sudden extremes in emotion can destroy a person. One minute you're up and the next you're down. It was exactly the same psychological torment we'd been through at Christmas. We were led to believe all of our worries would be over, only for everything to end up being an even worse nightmare.

Was this all just one big game to Commercide? Nick and his colleagues knew my mental health was precarious and that I'd tried to kill myself and been admitted for psychiatric help on more than one occasion. They knew that planting all this confusion and fear in my head would send me over the edge. They had to be behind all this craziness but there was no way of proving it.

At this point I would have preferred that someone would come and shoot me because at least this extreme stress would all be over. It was Chinese torture. Every cell in my body was constantly being triggered by shock and distress.

I told John we had to tell the police what was happening. We needed protection. John tried to reassure me that I was overthinking everything and needed to have some faith that common sense and truth would prevail. I tried to quiet my mind even though my head was spinning with possible scenarios.

The next day I wrote everything down so I wouldn't forget Paul's words. There were odd things he said during his two hour-long visit that preyed on my mind. Who exactly was this guy?

I looked at his TikTok account and saw he had just posted a new video of himself standing outside the museum in Scunthorpe telling everyone he'd recently arrived home after visiting a friend. It looked like he was reassuring whoever had sent him that he had completed his mission. John and I decided to wait until Monday to speak to him again. This time we decided that we'd record the phone call.

That same Monday morning we received an email from Commercide's lawyers insisting that we stopped fighting them and accepted their terms to get the matter over with. I mentioned it to Paul on the phone and he asked why didn't we just do that.

I explained that withdrawing our legal action meant we would have to pay Commercide's legal fees and we were running out of money. We had no choice but to push ahead with our claim and make sure we won.

Paul was adamant that I talked to the spiritual healer he'd mentioned before. He said she'd give me good advice and would take payments over the phone. There was no way I was giving my bank card details to someone I didn't know. Did he really think I was such a fool?

I pushed him to confirm if what he'd said about Commercide dropping their lawsuit against us was true. My voice was shaking because I was so desperate to hear evidence that he was part of their scheme and present it to the police. Of course, he didn't give me a direct answer.

"Like I said, it doesn't work like that. You know what, I need to talk to my healer friend myself because I don't know if I've told you too much. I'll speak to her, then I'll get back to you later today. Calm down, you sound upset," he said patronisingly.

"I'm actually stronger and more determined than ever," I countered, bluffing like a poker player.

I put the phone down, shaking with a mixture of frustration and adrenalin. It took me a few hours to calm down. On reflection, I was proud of myself for demanding answers. I waited anxiously to hear back from Paul even though deep down I knew that my head was being fucked with. Later that day he sent me the following text:

"Sorry Sharon, I can't help you. The best thing you can do is follow your instincts. I wish you well."

CAPITAL PUNISHMENT

CHAPTER 19

The Police Do Nothing Again

After the phone call with the Freemason, John and I decided to ask one of our friends to video us while we described everything that had happened to us. The police hadn't been interested in looking at the proof we'd given them to show we were being threatened and psychologically terrorised.

I'd given them all the evidence months ago. They had photos, CCTV footage, texts and recordings. Enough was enough. I decided to go and see them again. I arrived at the police station expecting it to be busy but there was nobody at reception. Eventually a policewoman came out of a side door.

"Do you have an appointment?" she asked.

What? I needed an appointment to report a serious crime? I told her I didn't but it was a serious matter.

"What's the nature of your complaint?"

I wasn't prepared for this. I'm sure that what I blurted out sounded quite ridiculous.

I explained that I had been visited by a man claiming to be a Freemason who had indirectly threatened me. Then I told her about the woman who pretended to want to buy our house and had strung us along for months. It was my understanding that it was all part of a wider conspiracy orchestrated by a private equity firm to stop me and my husband defending ourselves against the fabricated lawsuit they'd launched against us in order to steal our business and profit from the sale of my house and I urgently needed to speak to someone because we were being terrorised.

The policewoman's expression clearly showed she thought I was unhinged and was trying to work out if I was on drugs or just mentally ill. She took my number and said someone would call me. I sat outside the police station and waited for half an hour until an officer came to see me. She wasn't in uniform so I presumed she was a detective.

It took me an hour and a half to go through all the details again. I told her John and I had recorded everything and gave her a memory stick with all the evidence. I also left Paul's bag with the candle and other bits with her but she didn't even take a statement.

"Leave it with me. I'll come back to you when I've spoken to my boss," she said, leaving me sitting in the side room.

About 20 minutes later she returned to tell me that they would look into it and someone would be in touch. Then she continued, but now talking to me as if I was a child, warning, "You shouldn't give people on TikTok your phone number and you definitely shouldn't let strangers into your home."

Are you kidding me? Did I need to be shot and killed before they took action?

The system has broken down since the lockdowns. Unless you have knocked out a granny and stolen her handbag or said the wrong thing on WhatsApp nothing much else is considered a crime. Complicated cases involving lies, mind games and threats were too much of a challenge for the average cop. Despite them promising to get back to me I heard nothing of any relevance. I called to ask for an update but nobody could give me any information.

What about Paul, the Freemason/healer who had come to my house and told me that "they" could take me out from two miles away? What about the threat he made when he told me that if I spoke out my life would be at risk? Why hadn't the police interviewed him?

I now believe he told us the story about the events of 9/11 and the bomb at Euro Disney to make me sound crazy when I reported everything. His tactic had worked.

It had taken me a lot of courage to speak to the police in the first place, but now I am bitter about the way everything was handled. I'd call and explain my frustration at being passed to the same traffic cop. Then I would be appeased and assured someone would deal with my complaint and get transferred back to the same voicemail box.

On one occasion I was in tears from sheer frustration. This prompted someone to say that my case had been passed to international intelligence, but I was just being humoured. Once again, I was transferred to the same recorded message.

I contacted Citizens' Advice to see if there was any legal facility that could help me put together a defence for my upcoming court appearance. It was explained to me that policies had been changed during the Covid lockdowns. Now you have to fund your own legal action.

They suggested that I contact my local MP Nick Dakin. I sent him an email that Friday evening and was surprised to receive a response by Monday morning saying he was available to meet me for 40 minutes at my house that same week on Wednesday.

Nick arrived as promised. I had 40 minutes to describe Commercide's false accusations, how they'd stolen our business from under our feet and why there is a need for laws to prevent private equity firms from seizing businesses this way. I also told him about my encounters with the police and how frustrating the reporting process had been.

It was difficult having to explain everything within my allotted time-span because the picture was so complex with so many individually bizarre details that I had to be careful not to sound unhinged.

The MP said he had direct access to people who could provide me with some answers quickly and agreed that I needed to know what was going on because it was obviously causing me a great deal of distress. I was relieved that he seemed to understand what I was saying.

I had two further meetings with him where he gave me some updates on his progress. He did get a response from an MP telling him what I already knew from my own online search. The "reply" looked like the information was AI generated. He suggested another route I could explore, but I'd already tried that and had got nowhere.

CAPITAL PUNISHMENT

By this point I had researched everything in a desperate attempt to find someone who could help us, but every road came to a frustrating halt. I pride myself on my tenacity and have never given up fighting injustice, but this time I felt truly cornered.

I understand why so many people have taken their lives since the Covid lockdowns. I hadn't realised how the balance of power has shifted. There had definitely been some kind of reset and Big Government had stopped supporting the ordinary citizens of this world.

Many small businesses have been wiped out and the corporations have become bigger and more powerful. Their interests came first above all else. After the vaccine mandates and enforced quarantine - up to 17 months for some - respect for individual rights and freedoms seem to have all but disappeared.

Because I've had to repeat my story so often, writing this book is the best way to explain everything that has happened. It's such a complex and intricate saga with all the twists and turns of a spy novel. It has been a cathartic process and has helped me make sense of a lot of the seemingly inexplicable events.

When I read it over sometimes, I wonder how I haven't suffered a heart attack! It seems I have been constantly fighting a system that is so broken and so wrong. My family and friends all say they couldn't have done it and would have given up years ago.

I am so disheartened by the attacks that have been launched against us and the never-ending onslaught of financial and legal challenges and ask myself, "Why us?" It feels like a large chunk of my life and John's has been one long test.

I can now see clearly that the world isn't what I originally thought it was; I think everything is planned. During the lockdowns we saw so many things change. We used to live a different life where we knew where they stood, but now people are frightened about what's coming next.

You can't help but read about the conspiracies. I am not saying I believe all of them, but things are changing at a rapid speed and it all appears to be by design.

CHAPTER 20

My Stay at Haven House

After our visit from Paul the Freemason my mental health deteriorated drastically. My friend Rita came over in the morning with some sunflowers to cheer me up. She seemed surprised that the police weren't interested in following up on what looked to be an obvious gameplan. The complexity and subtlety of it meant that any attempt to describe what was going made me sound insane. Of course, that was the point.

Later that evening I scrutinised Freemason Paul's TikTok platform through suspicious eyes. In every post he displayed the numbers 777. He also wore a cross on a chain. I watched as he spoke live from his kitchen at his home in London. I thought he'd told us he lived in Wales? Then he set a vase in front of the camera.

"Look at these beautiful sunflowers I bought today," he smirked.

I woke John up and told him that there must be cameras in our house because Freemason Paul knew about the sunflowers Rita had given me earlier. We both watched his video repeatedly for an hour, but now the vase of flowers was nowhere to be seen. Would this Matrix movie ever end?

I called Paul my ex-SAS friend, but he didn't answer. He later sent me a text saying he was on holiday all week. I was desperate to speak to him. Being in the SAS he would know if the police should take our situation seriously. I even bought a burner phone because I didn't know who was listening in to my calls.

Eventually I got to talk to SAS Paul and updated him on the Freemason and the police's response but he just played everything down. He seemed unfazed by our visitor's sinister warnings and asked why I would let a perfect stranger into my house.

He said the guy was obviously a fruit cake and I should ignore him. His response echoed what seemed to be a common reaction. Minimise everything, accuse me of being paranoid and tell me I'd brought all the stress on myself.

John and I sat in shock. Were we imagining things? Were we actually going crazy? Had the pressure finally got to our heads and made us think everyone was out to get us?

No. Everything that had happened had been pre-meditated but we did not know exactly who was behind it all. Was it Commercide? Was it the Freemasons? Or was it some other agency we didn't know about? I didn't know who to trust any more.

I made an appointment at the doctors' office because my anxiety was at an all-time high. This was a living hell and I wished I could be seriously ill so I could keep my promise that I wouldn't take my life. You wouldn't let a dog suffer like this, never mind a human.

John and I were isolated with very few friends. The ones we did have avoided us like the plague because every conversation was dominated by the torment we were living in. It got to the point where I even questioned God and asked him why he had given me such a shit life full of constant worry.

John would sleep as soon as his head hit the pillow, but I would lie awake for hours stewing in my thoughts. We were living on a shoestring budget with no quality of life. My only escape was TikTok or the TV. I couldn't live in the moment or even see a future. There was no escape. Now I couldn't be on my own because of what the Freemason man had told us.

"They" were in the police, the government and even the health service. I was petrified and couldn't even go to the shops because my nerves were shot. The pain of living was too much. I told John I couldn't stand it anymore and begged him for permission to end my life.

John agreed to go with me for my doctor's appointment. I hoped that he'd give me some sleeping pills and antidepressants which would help me recover. But when I explained how bad I was feeling, instead of focusing on me the doctor turned to John and said, "Don't I remember you from last year when you were selling your business?"

I thought it was crazy that he remembered John from a routine appointment all that time ago but somehow didn't remember him from a few months earlier when he had been struggling to eat, had horrendous stomach pains and had nearly died!

I'd even told this doctor something was seriously wrong. Surely, he'd remember that? John had passed blood and I'd asked him if it could be cancer. He looked at me with disdain and spoke to me in such a patronising way.

His exact words were, "Calm down. Let's not get ahead of ourselves. I'll put him on the fast track for investigation." It's not so much what he said as the way he looked at me and the way he said it. He treated me like I was being hysterical.

How could he think I was overreacting? We had visited A & E three times and even after a full body scan nobody spotted the problem. The doctors even thought it was just a chest infection! The last time they sent him home a surgeon had checked his scans and said he was happy that there was nothing seriously wrong with him.

I knew my husband. If he said he felt bad it was usually when he was facing a life-or-death situation, other than that he never complained. For my own piece of mind, I asked if the scans could be sent to John's consultant in Leeds who knew his history well, because that's where he'd had all his surgeries.

Within 24 hours his surgeon in Leeds had called John to tell him all the arteries to his stomach were completely blocked and only one could potentially be saved. This was a life-threatening situation. He had to pack a bag, not eat any food and be prepared for emergency surgery.

To hear this doctor recall his meeting with John from the previous year but not from a few weeks ago sent my paranoia into overdrive. Omg! Did they misdiagnose his condition on purpose? Did the doctor know we'd been accused of fraud? I needed to get out of there!

I asked him for some sleeping tablets and some antidepressants because I was suicidal. The doctor looked at John and asked if he would look after the tablets.

At that moment I was reminded of Nick's words, "And don't think you can take the suicidal route…" Of course I wasn't going to be given the pills. Despite John's assurances that he'd keep the tablets under lock and key, the doctor prescribed propranolol which is a beta blocker. I couldn't get out of that room quickly enough.

Because I was still a wreck and John was scared that the pills wouldn't help, he took me straight to A & E. Their crisis team assessed me and I was told I could either go home and wait until the intervention staff called to put me on a managed plan. Or I could be admitted into Haven House, a public funded safe house. Alternatively, I could go to Great Oaks, an NHS mental health care unit in Scunthorpe for seven days. I knew I couldn't go home, so I chose to go to Great Oaks.

We waited while they did the paperwork. When the administrator returned, she said I would have to go to their Leicester facility because there were no spaces at Scunthorpe. I panicked. I couldn't be miles away and isolated even more. Money was tight, so John wouldn't be able to visit me every day and he was the only person in the world I trusted. So, I said I'd go home if they gave me some sleeping tablets.

I tried to calm down at home but it was hopeless. My mind was racing and I couldn't tolerate the intense anxiety. I went back to A & E the following day and asked to go to Haven House. They gave me all the necessary paperwork and we went home so I could grab some clothes. I was petrified and sobbed all the way there. I knew I was ill, but I was so angry with Nick and the rest of the predators at Commercide for putting me there in the first place.

CAPITAL PUNISHMENT

At 4:00am we arrived at the facility which was just a basic house in the middle of town. It was warm and I instantly felt safe. Two members of staff greeted us and went through all the house rules. I can't really remember the first couple of days because I was given sleeping pills and slept through most of it.

The next day I had a shower. It was the first one I'd had in weeks. When you don't want to live, looking after yourself is the last thing you care about. But I stuck to my promise and wouldn't attempt to take my life again. I couldn't see how a few days in this place would make me feel any better, but I'd try anything to feel better than I did now.

Haven House is a godsend when you are in a crisis. I can't praise the people there enough for the care they gave me at my time of need. There were always two members of staff on call night and day, so I always felt secure. My racing thoughts eventually calmed down. It was just what I needed: a break from the world, so I could put things in perspective and breathe.

If I compare their staff to those at The Priory I'd honestly say they're just as good, if not better. The Priory costs somewhere in the region of £1,000 a day. The only difference is that it offers optional programmes to help you understand your mental health issues better. I believe Haven House is funded by the Mind charity and donations.

A large part of the therapy involved in recovery is talking. You have to offload everything that has brought you there. As they say, it's good to talk. I was lucky because I was the only person there for most of my stay and had access to the staff at any time day or night.

During my time in the house a nurse would check my vitals and blood tests and an ECG were done at the local hospital. Five days later I felt like a new person. My confidence was back, my mind was rested and I had the courage to keep going.

I also spoke to a therapist who devised a follow-up plan before I left. Everyone spoke highly of a particular psychiatrist and I was told he would be coming to see me. However, a different one was sent, in addition to a junior doctor.

This psychiatrist told me he wanted to put me on an antipsychotic drug to stop my mind from racing. I presume he'd heard about the bizarre things that had happened to me and thought I was a paranoid schizophrenic and completely delusional.

I proceeded to show him all the evidence that what I was saying was true and told him I had recordings, video footage and texts to back up everything I'd been through. All the staff believed what I said, but the psychiatrist was convinced that my imagination was running riot.

He told me, "We want you to take these tablets, but I have to inform you they are really bad for you." Up until that point I had felt safe, but now I couldn't shake off the bad feelings this man gave me. I just wanted to leave.

The next day an appointment was made for me to see the other highly recommended psychiatrist at Haven House. John came with me because I still had trust issues and he wanted to support me in any way he could. When we got there a nurse explained they were running late but the psychiatrist wouldn't be long.

An hour and a half past my appointment time, I was finally taken to the consulting room only to find the same psychiatrist that I'd had seen before waiting for me. He explained that unfortunately the other one couldn't make it. I cried through the whole consultation. I had such a bad feeling about this guy.

He said he had read all the notes the staff at Haven House had prepared and was still convinced that I needed the antipsychotic medication. I felt so deflated. I didn't want to seem like a troublemaker, so I didn't say anything about having to take the pills.

As soon as we stepped outside, I looked at John. He said I know what you're thinking. During our meeting he had called him Paul four times! That's why I had sobbed all the way through.

Then I thought, "Omg!" The Freemason man's words suddenly came to mind: "They are in the health service, they're everywhere." Could it really be true?

After this I decided I had to advocate for myself, so I insisted that my next appointment should be with the other psychiatrist that everyone had said good things about. He was lovely, kind and knowledgeable. He had obviously read my file and was able to ask me a lot of relevant questions.

In his opinion I had ADHD and was suffering from trauma and most probably PTSD. He suggested I had talking therapy until I received a diagnosis from a specialist doctor, but that would take a minimum of 18 months because they were so far behind. I didn't need the diagnosis or the label and was fine with waiting my turn.

He explained that in the meantime, my care plan would be managed by the psychiatrist who thought I was psychotic. I explained that he had called my husband Paul four times and that was a massive trigger for me. I asked if he could manage my follow-up care but it was to no avail.

Four weeks later I had my first video call with another therapist. No guesses for what that guy's name was. Yes. Paul. I cried all the way through that meeting too. I couldn't let them do this to me.

I researched ways of dealing with ADHD and devised my own coping mechanisms. Now I knew why I was, the way I was I could do more to help myself. I knew my frustrations made me angry. Instead of exploding and saying terrible things, I breathed and took time to process the situation and ask myself if this was my mind or just a temporary worry.

I started to meditate and focus on the things that helped my brain work better. I cut out sugar and ate simple food like meat and two veg. I walked outside in the fresh air and appreciated the nature all around us. It was just all the basics that I'd forgotten having been stuck in a state of turmoil for so long. I also started yoga and poured everything out by writing this book which has helped me come to terms with everything that has happened.

A few weeks later I received a call to arrange another appointment. I was told this one was important because they had a new care plan for me. I didn't want to go. Since I'd focused on my own recovery I felt more at peace. Our legal battles with Buildadeck were on hold until the next part of the process and I was feeling like my life was getting back on track.

CAPITAL PUNISHMENT

I met with a lovely counsellor called Trish. She said I had been passed to her and her team who specialised in treating psychosis. I was fuming! The original psychiatrist was still managing my care plan, but I kept calm and went along with what they suggested. If they thought they could help I had nothing to lose.

The following week John and I met two of the specialists who asked me a series of questions which I answered honestly. Within ten minutes they both stopped and looked at each other. Then one said, "I know you're thinking what I am thinking. She's not psychotic. They both agreed I had been traumatised and understood that everything I had told them was factual and not imaginary.

I felt so relieved. It was a long session during which I cried many tears. We discussed my childhood and my achievements and the ridiculous situations life had thrown at me recently. For the first time I had hope. The counsellors said they would speak to the psychiatrist and inform him of their opinion.

A few days later Trish called to say they had held a big meeting about me and it was decided that I would be staying with the psychotic team for another three months. I had weekly meetings with specialists who wanted to get to know me better. The meetings were soon switched to fortnightly when they saw my speedy progress. I'd sit with Trish and a nurse called Paula and chat about my past. They made me feel relaxed, so I talked freely and even laughed again.

During my final week I was informed that I'd suffered a series of traumas and needed trauma recovery, but the waiting list for help was very long. But they assured me that I would not be passed back to the psychiatrist and his team.

CAPITAL PUNISHMENT

Meanwhile, I contemplated why the name Paul triggered me.

My fellow director and business partner was called Paul.

The ex-SAS guy who introduced me to the production companies was called Paul.

The Freemason "healer" was called Paul and his girlfriend was Pauline.

The psychiatrist called my husband Paul four times during my assessment.

The guy I saw for talking therapy was called Paul.

Was it all a coincidence? Or was it one big game designed to tip me over the edge? If it wasn't, then all I can say is fate had conspired against me in the most outlandish way. I know it will make me sound crazy if I mention all this again, but for someone in a heightened state of vigilance, it was a pattern that was impossible to ignore.

CAPITAL PUNISHMENT

CHAPTER 21

More Warnings to "Let it Go"

I decided to document everything that had happened and analyse it to see if there was some kind of method to the madness. A coincidence is defined as two similar but unrelated events. Therefore, it is impossible to have a pattern of coincidences.

For example, why was everyone involved in our ordeal called Paul? Or Pauline? What about Paul, the Freemason/healer who told me "they" could take me out from two miles away and that if I spoke out about Commercide my life would be at risk?

Was his symbolic message with the vase full of sunflowers on TikTok meant to tell us we were being watched? Why did he want to make us believe our house would be sold and Commercide wanted to settle?

It certainly felt like someone was trying to taunt us into madness and despair. My existence seemed to be one of constant mental and physical pain. I'd endured over a year of pure torture and was exhausted.

I informed my ex-SAS friend Paul that I had filmed over two and a half hours of footage explaining everything I had been through. It was for my own protection because I was convinced something bad was going to happen to me. I couldn't even leave the house without feeling intense anxiety and I didn't dare go anywhere near my daughter Molly or her kids in case I put them in danger too.

The only way to protect myself was to give copies of the video to Rita, Sue and others that I won't name for their own protection. They had seen me suffer and promised me that if I faced anything sinister, they would scream and shout loudly about it on my behalf.

Then I got a barrage of text messages from SAS Paul who was still on holiday. He warned me not to jeopardise my legal case and said he had no idea what was going on with all the different Pauls, the fake house buyer, the weird warnings and bizarre coincidences. It all sounded completely whacko.

"What do you think a judge would think hearing all this for the first time?" he wrote.

"They would wonder if you were fit to stand trial. Commercide will probably use your hospitalisations for when you had your mental breakdowns for stress and your eating disorder to prove you are mentally unstable."

I replied that my hospital stays were a reaction to trauma and I wasn't mentally ill. Plus, it was common knowledge that John and I had been accused of theft and fraud but we hadn't been given the chance to tell our side of the story or talk about all the weird things that had been happening to us.

His exact message was, "Do not go down a conspiracy theory rabbit hole. Deal with the problem at hand and get yourself operational in business again."

I couldn't believe what I was seeing. How dare he tell me to start again! I was a 55-year-old who was about to retire. John and I had been living within our means, growing the company and working up to 14-hour days until the time we could sell our shares (which were worth millions) and spend the rest of our days living quietly and comfortably together.

Now our funds were running out. I couldn't sell my house. Plus, there was a chance it could be stolen from me because someone had invented a pile of lies accusing me of theft! There was no way I was going to allow this to happen. I couldn't just walk away.

"Don't release any videos online," SAS Paul warned.

I told him I could not allow this corrupt, opportunistic private equity company to get away with what they were doing.

"So, there's a need to have legislation," he stated.

"Yes," I said.

"Now you're talking the right kind of language," he responded.

Was he another one who was undercover and on some kind of mission? Couldn't he see I was being subjected to an orchestrated effort to demoralise me and break me down? I felt like I was going crazy. I just wanted to go to sleep and never wake up.

Later that day I received an email from Natalie at the TV production company. She sent me a message with a video clip attached to it. I thought it would be a personal message from her, but it turned out to be a 40-second segment from a longer recording.

The footage concerned the doctor Michael Mosley who'd disappeared while on holiday in Cyprus. It had been all over the news channels. They had spent days looking for him before eventually finding him lying on some rocks after allegedly having a heart attack.

There were rumours that he was about to do an expose on the Covid vaccine telling everyone that these mRNA shots caused a deadly replication of the spike protein which caused massive inflammation throughout the body as well as heart problems in previously young, healthy adults. Some say his death was no accident.

I sat there shaking. Why had Natalie sent this video to me? Was it a threat that I would end up in the same way? I was so angry I sent her this email:

"Hi Natalie, you just sent me this. I don't know if this is a warning to keep my mouth shut. But I am speaking my truth regardless. I'm not scared."

CHAPTER 22

Am I Just Experiencing Everyone's Future?

In my last book "Mother of Invention," I wrote about my old house in Scunthorpe being broken into back in 2009. My phone and laptop were stolen and my car was set alight with petrol. A few days before the break in, I noticed someone standing outside the French doors at the back of my house while I was alone. I was doing the final amendments to the book I was writing about my experiences on "Dragons' Den."

It was pitch black outside but I could see someone's eyes staring at me. I froze to the spot, unable to break my gaze with this figure. I couldn't even grab my phone and call the police.

My heart was racing a million miles an hour. You would have thought this person would run when he knew he'd been spotted, but he didn't. He just stood there with his eyes fixed on me. A few days later, this same lurker broke into my house and set fire to my car!

A couple of weeks went by and a policeman came to my house to inform me that they had recovered my phone and laptop but were keeping them until the court hearing. I asked who had stolen them and was told they were found at the home of a policeman who lived nearby.

Around a month later, my property was returned. I was told the case had been dropped and I should just move on with my life and forget the theft and arson had ever happened! The laptop contained an unedited but almost complete version of my book. Luckily, I had sent a copy to a good friend of mine who now lives in California.

In the early days of Magnamole Karina had helped design the packaging for my product. It's harder than you think because you have to convey what they do as quickly as possible. So, she designed a logo that incorporated the magnetic element of the tool. Out of the kindness of her heart she helped me during the early stages of my business right through to the end.

When she moved to the US we kept in touch and even though we can go years and years without contacting each other, if I reached out for support it was as if the last time I spoke with her was yesterday.

Now she writes books herself as well as ghost writing for others and has offered to edit mine. Her talents are never ending and she is one person in my life I believe you meet for a reason.

Karina sent me the copy of the Stanford Law Document which outlines how the unscrupulous private equity companies set out to reduce entrepreneurism down into dust. These investors, who are described as "vultures" or "predators," take a disproportionate share of the company for minimal investment then exploit its vulnerabilities for their own gain.

These cases rarely reach the courts. Even if they do, the identity of these investment firms is disguised. So even if they lose their legal action, they will just close down the company they destroyed and go off to suck the life out of another one, crippling it with debt, enforcing impossible targets and changing the terms of any agreements on a whim.

Any business owner who has experienced the trauma of such an experience can never feel at peace in the world again. The shame of the accusations and the disbelief that such injustices remain unchallenged are unresolved pains they have to live with. Many have committed suicide while others have settled out of court just to make the nightmare go away. Then there are the few that choose to stand their ground like me and Tiffany Cianci.

But taking on this fight has come at a huge price, literally and metaphorically. John and I have lost a lot of friends because of it. The complexity and scariness of our situation has frightened many of them away because it hints at a far more sinister picture of what is really going on in the world.

Unfortunately, the vast majority of people do not want to educate themselves on politics or social issues. Since the lockdowns people are either aware of things like The New World Order and Agenda 2030 or they have no idea what these objectives mean and are not interested in knowing. They just bury their heads in the sand because they don't know what to do.

The New World Order or Great Reset which the World Economic Forum has established as a blueprint for the future of the world and may be a good thing in some ways, but all the signs indicate that the globalist agenda will mean absolute government control and the ownership of literally everything on earth will be placed in the hands of a few mega billionaires.

Even nature itself is being modified and genetically engineered to create patentable products that would never evolve naturally. The globalists are playing God and are recreating the world into a revised format where only people who serve their purpose will be allowed to experience life.

My eyes have been opened to the system that is purposely designed to eliminate small businesses as well as making the ownership of property and the acquisition of wealth more difficult with each generation. Yes, ultimately, we "will own nothing" as the globalists have forewarned.

With a greatly reduced population entirely dependent on government handouts this is the bleak and soul-crushing future that lies ahead for the people who are left. It truly makes me feel this world country has been taken over from within.

Oppression of basic freedoms, propaganda delivered by the corporate media disguised as "news" and massive social engineering via immigration is now the norm. It's all being rolled out under the banner of sustainability, diversity, equality and "democracy."

Like George Orwell's 1984, we are living in a world where the truth can be bought and liars are rewarded for promoting the interests of the multinational corporations. The government's main goal is to take our money and put it into the hands of these private firms and the handful of multi-billionaires that own them, as quickly and slickly as possible. Unfortunately, the facilitators of this scheme who think they'll earn a privileged place in the world that's to come will sadly find they are "useless" and expendable, like everyone else.

To ensure the global "elite" retain and expand their dominance over the rest of us, a digital control grid is quietly being built to track each person and control everyone's financial transactions. Basically, if you don't comply with their rules, they will turn off your money. You won't have a voice in this digital gulag. There will be no appeal, no recourse and no alternative. And no. This is not a "conspiracy theory." It's being enforced in real time, right now.

Look what happened to the Canadian truckers. Their bank accounts were frozen – and their friends and supporters also had their accounts frozen – when the establishment objected to them protesting against the vaccine mandates.

Like I said, most people are blind to what's going on and think anyone who speaks out about the dystopian way things are going is an unhinged extreme right wing conspiracy theorist. They are brainwashed by the official narrative of the media conglomerates who are run by a handful of individuals who are prominent figures at the World Economic Forum.

People who dare to shine a light on what's going on are shunned, smeared or cancelled altogether. We have seen this time and again where doctors have lost their medical licenses for questioning the safety of vaccines, social media accounts have been shut down or shadow banned for "wrong think." People have been arrested, killed and "suicided" for exposing the lies that shape our perception of the world.

There is now a huge divide between those who are brave and "awake" and speak out about the crap we're being told and those who prefer to hide among the anonymity of the flock of sheep. As the saying goes, "The only thing evil needs to triumph is for good people to do nothing."

It gives me comfort to know that I am among a growing community who believe strongly that truth must be distinguished from lies and evil should be called out for what it is. Which brings me to my next example of corporate greed, whereby the wrongdoer deflects blame and evades liability by countersuing the victims of their injustice or dragging out the legal process.

CHAPTER 23

Our House Build from Hell

We were full of optimism and hope when we engaged an architect we knew to design a new home for us in 2021. It was the most important project of our lives and we were confident that our good friend Declan Amble, the founder of Amble Architecture, would come up with an open-plan concept that would not be out of place on the TV show "Grand Designs."

We'd known Declan since the early 2000s and John had worked with him before. He had his quirks and was known for being hot-headed and lackadaisical at times, but he was a brilliant architect who had designed many large commercial buildings. So, we trusted that he would easily be able to handle our relatively small project.

Our connection to Declan went deeper than just our professional ties. He was also married to the sister of my brother's former wife and it was through him that John and I first met. When I told Declan I was looking for investors for my Magnamole invention he introduced us. All this history and the family ties made us feel confident he would have our best interests at heart.

Having lived in older buildings before, we decided to do something different this time and have a sleek, contemporary house built from industrial materials with tons of glass to make the most of the panoramic views across Alkborough Flats and the Trent and Ouse rivers.

It would have high ceilings, a large living/kitchen area and lots of high-end features. To help realise this vision we created mood boards and even built a polystyrene model to give an idea of the kind of structure we had in mind. All the architects had to do was to take our ideas and make them work from a technical and structural perspective.

In August 2021 we sent Declan an email outlining the key design elements, which included a frameless glass cornered window on one side of the living room to maximise the view and create a seamless living space to the outdoors. There would be a bath in one of the bedrooms with a view of the river and a large terrace/balcony outside the two first floor bedrooms.

We spent a long time planning the layout and were sure everything would run smoothly because we were in good hands, or so we thought. Despite all this pre-planning we didn't anticipate just how quickly things would unravel.

At first, the delays were small. A copyright notice was missed on one of the drawings submitted to the planning department. This cost us a month's delay. Then other silly things like an unread email here and a missed text message there started to add up, setting us back even further.

In April 2022 we had problems with the structural insulated panels. There were delays getting construction drawings to the manufacturer and when the panels finally arrived, they were the wrong size. This wasn't just frustrating; it was expensive. Every mistake meant more time, more labour and more money that we hadn't budgeted for.

By the Autumn the design flaws and the downtimes on the build had become impossible to ignore. The original build time was suggested by the architect to be 9 to 12 months. It was now May 2025 and the house still wasn't finished.

Another major issue was the window placements. Declan had delegated our project to his design team. Someone at Amble Architecture had decided that the windows should sit between the steel beams. But when the time came to install them, it became clear that this wasn't structurally feasible.

The windows could not sit on the steelwork as it was designed as this would have put them between the steel uprights. This would have allowed the cold to transfer from the outside of the steel into the house: a phenomenon known as "thermal bridging." In order to move the windows to the outside of the columns additional steel had to be welded to the existing steel. This resulted in further delays and additional costs

Then came the roof debacle. We had assumed Declan would have personally checked to ensure everything was designed correctly. It never crossed our minds that the roof would become such a catastrophic issue because nobody had spotted an obvious error.

Amble Architecture had originally proposed installing a "warm roof" which was something we had not seen in any of their previous designs or even discussed with them. This would have meant having a step down from one area of the terrace to another and bi-folding doors to one bedroom and not both as we had originally wanted.

We had no choice but to reject that idea and have the plans redrawn. This back-and-forth over the roof redesign stretched over several months. We chased the architects for drawings, questioned the ventilation issues and watched in disbelief as deadlines came and went. The solution they finally came up with was a "cold roof" which was something we didn't fully understand at the time but would soon come to realise was going to be extremely problematic.

At this point, John and I were exhausted both financially and emotionally. What had started as an exciting, life-changing project had turned into an ever-spiralling nightmare. The costs far exceeded our original budget and with every setback we felt more dejected. There were days when we questioned how we had ended up here again: trusting people who promised they'd look after us and then failed to deliver on their promises.

Beyond the financial cost, the personal strain was immense. The delays, the financial uncertainty and the constant battles took a toll on our health and our relationship. Arguments became frequent, sleep was elusive and our once hopeful dream was now a source of constant anxiety.

Due to the architect dragging his feet, things going wrong and costs spinning out of control I had a breakdown and spent the whole of October 2022 in The Priory in Cheltenham recovering from the stress.

In January 2023 building control confirmed that the cold roof design would not work. The steel structure blocked the necessary airflow, leading to the risk of condensation which would eventually lead to structural damage. The architect's proposal was to drill holes in the steel beams to allow air to pass through. Everyone thought the idea was absurd.

In February 2023, after yet another delay, Amble Architecture finally admitted defeat. They proposed a new hybrid warm roof solution which should have been

designed from the start. The drawings were produced in March but the damage was done. We'd spent more than we could afford, endured months of unnecessary delays and had lost our enthusiasm for our supposed "dream home."

To make matters worse, immediately after we were sacked from Buildadeck in April 2023, all the contractors were told we were being investigated for fraud. News spread around the village because some of them lived there too. Not only were we subjected to the embarrassment of trying to defend ourselves against Commercide's vile allegations, we had to pay some of the contractors up front so they'd continue with the build.

Even today, our house still remains unfinished with wires hanging down from the walls and ceilings. A glass balustrade for the stairs and a lift which John needs to get to the first floor have yet to be installed.

Looking back, the signs had been there: the lapses in attention to detail, the missed deadlines, the assumptions that had been made without proper checks. When you trust someone, especially someone you have a history with and was a part of your extended family, you don't expect them to let you down this badly.

The financial burden of those mistakes still weighs on us. The emotional toll even more so. What should have been the creation of something beautiful became a battle to reclaim control over something that had slipped through our fingers. Once again, we were left wondering how had it come to this?

Because the architects would not assume responsibility for any of the structural issues, we had no choice but to start legal proceedings and sue them for breach of contract and the £500,000 plus that it has cost us to fix all the problems caused by their incompetence. We also added an additional sum for all the pain and suffering we have endured.

Of course, Amble Architecture is fighting us at every turn. They've deployed every dirty tactic imaginable: stalling on document submissions, requesting unnecessary extensions and focusing on procedural technicalities in a deliberate ploy to complicate matters and slow things down. It's exhausting and disheartening, but we refuse to back down.

As we have dug deeper, we've uncovered more unsettling details. Amble Architecture' professional indemnity insurers – who we assumed would take responsibility – are a British company in name, but they are owned by yet another American private equity investment firm. Their modus operandi is not one of fairness or resolution, but of minimising and eliminating payouts and protecting their bottom line.

This realisation has only fuelled our determination to take our battle to the courts. We are not just fighting for ourselves anymore. We are fighting to expose a system that allows professionals in this field to operate with impunity, shielded by corporate layers that put profits over people.

As we continue to defend ourselves against yet another injustice, we often wonder how different our lives would be if the project had gone as planned. We'd be living peacefully in the countryside in a beautifully designed modern home. But instead, we are stuck in a relentless struggle trying to hold people accountable for their failures. Worse than that, we are surrounded by reminders of our situation as we have to live in this unfinished house which I have now come to hate.

Our fight is not just about reclaiming what we have lost, it is about ensuring the same thing does not happen to others. The existing legislation, adept as it may be in providing housebuilders with protection and speedy dispute resolution, fails people like us who are building a house to live in, not to sell.

There are two main reasons I am talking about this during our litigation with Commercide Ventures. First, it was agreed with all the directors at Buildadeck that some of the building materials could be more cost effectively purchased through the company.

I know I am repeating myself but I really must make the following points clear. Everyone knew the payments for these materials would be allocated against my deferred consideration (the money Commercide still owed me four years after the "sale" of my installation business to them). In fact, I was owed in the region of £300,000 even after spending around £150,000 on materials over a period of 14 months.

Every invoice had my personal home address on it, so it was clearly identified as relating to my house build. Two separate authorised people at Buildadeck also accounted for every purchase and the person who paid the invoice recorded the transaction on file to avoid any allegations of misconduct.

During this time, Commercide had total access to all Buildadeck's accounts and banking records. Their independent financial expert was also aware that the money owed to me was gradually being reduced and the management accounts clearly show this information. While preparing for the sale of Buildadeck, one of the largest international accountancy firms in the country did a full audit of the business.

As I mentioned before, Amble Architecture's insurers and their lawyers have deliberately caused delays to stretch the process out. The courts are also two years behind due to the pandemic. Every day that we are denied resolution puts even more pressure on our finances.

We had a report done by a reputable firm of construction experts who identified all the aspects of the build that were wrongly designed by the architects. We submitted this to them and after months of waiting they said they would have their own professionals carry out a survey and meet with our expert. We were told not to be at the house when they both arrived.

A few weeks later we spoke to the builder to prepare for mediation. He'd spoken to the structural engineer who agreed that Amble Architecture had caused all the issues. Interestingly, the structural engineer told the builder someone at Buildadeck had asked if our settlement could be delayed because he believed we'd use it to set ourselves up in business in competition against them. I was shocked when the builder told me it was common knowledge that we were being investigated for fraud.

The mediation was not successful. That is all I am allowed to say on that subject.

The legal back and forth still continues to this day, along with all the long delays. I cannot see the matter being resolved until the end of 2025 at the earliest. There is another hearing on May 28th 2025 with the architect. This was originally scheduled for January, but the day before the hearing Amble Architecture applied to have it delisted.

On 20th March 2025 we received a very long and complex letter from Den Architect's solicitors saying our complaint against them "failed to inform our client of the case it has to meet… being vague, confused, self-contradictory, insufficiently particularised and containing large amounts of irrelevant material and is in places simply incoherent or meaningless."

Consequently, they made an application to make us rewrite our claim because they couldn't understand any of it and it needed to be more concise and properly laid out in numbered paragraphs. They accused us of using AI generated material and lacking evidence to support our claim. They also warned us that we would end up having to pay substantial legal costs if they succeeded in their application to strike out our claims against them and would be willing to accept £20,000 to avoid the hearing on May 28th 2025.

All the evidence of their incompetence is clearly laid out in their own expert's report which is pretty damning. Basically, they are using diversionary, nit-picking tactics to keep this report away from the judge.

After having spent £2.2 million on the build, our house was valued by two independent estate agents at £2.5 million in 2023. Since then, we have received another offer of £2.2 million. We were honest with the prospective purchasers and told them we were suing the architect's firm for half a million pounds and whatever we won in court it was only fair to pass that on to them.

Sometime in August 2024 we went to their house for drinks to tell them about our offer. It was a few days after the billionaire Mike Lynch's super yacht had sunk in Sicily causing everyone on board to drown. He founded "Invoke Ventures," a private equity firm which invested in and supported technology companies.

He had spent years fighting legal battles related to the sale of his company as well as accusations of fraud and had been acquitted on all counts in June. Two months later he was dead. Mike Lynch's business partner and co-defendant Stephen Chamberlain was also killed in August 2024 after a car struck him while he was out running.

The prospective buyer asked us what we thought about both of these men dying at virtually the same time. I said I thought it was suspicious. Some people were calling their deaths "authorised non-judicial executions." Our host was adamant they were just unrelated accidents.

Now my hackles were up. I looked John in the eye and wondered if he was thinking the same as me. Was this guy yet another fake house buyer sent to deliver a covert warning from Commercide?

CAPITAL PUNISHMENT

Later that evening we told these "would-be buyers" about our troubles at Buildadeck. I also explained to them why we were involved in litigation with the house. Our host didn't seem fazed and went on to tell us that one of his best friends worked for JP Morgan and another buddy worked at Netflix. He described how the super-rich lived in a kind of annexed, parallel world and mingled in the same circles.

Shortly after this meeting, they sent someone to survey our house and their offer went down to £1.5 million. Once again, I felt hopeless and angry. The vultures continued to circle…

CAPITAL PUNISHMENT

CHAPTER 24

This Time John Gives Up

A year had almost gone by. According to the terms of the Settlement agreement we were now free to pursue other avenues to bring in some income. We were wondering about our next steps and considering moving abroad when one of John's old colleagues, Dan Jones from Buildadeck suggested they set up another decking business together. I was happy to use the money from my insurance claim against the architect (when I eventually received it) to help them get things off the ground.

We planned to discuss everything after we got back from a much-needed week-long holiday. On our return, John met with Dan to discuss the location of their unit, salaries and other details. To our dismay he admitted he'd told the directors of Buildadeck about his intentions to start a rival business and they had offered him a large bonus if he waited another eight months before doing anything, which he accepted.

John had been friends with Dan for a long time and took this betrayal very personally. It was the first time I had to step up and support him. He'd been cheated out of millions at Safestyle and Buildadeck and now his friend had seen an opportunity to make some quick cash and had done a deal with the devil. It was John's turn to question his purpose in life and whether the struggle was worth it.

That night he decided to drink. He rarely touches alcohol now except for the occasional glass of wine a few times a year. I watched him disintegrate as the booze drenched his mind in bitterness and self-pity. Finally, he cried that he'd had enough and didn't want to live any longer.

Now I had to be the strong one. It was my turn to grab all the tablets in the house and hide them. I felt so helpless and scared hearing him begging me for permission to let him go. John has always been my rock and I took it for granted that he would always be the logical strong one. This was a side of him I'd never seen before. He had totally given up.

No matter what I said, the alcohol just heightened all the negative emotions that had been building up inside him. He pleaded with me to join him and said we should end our lives together. He couldn't see any hope for the future and it was time to end the suffering and disappear into endless sleep.

I called my friend Rita for help because I was unable to get through to him. She jumped in her car and rushed straight over. She had not been there long when she told me to go to the shop and buy him some cigarettes. I hid all the medications from the house in the car and took them with me. Thankfully we were able to bring him down and eventually he fell asleep.

After this, John needed regular counselling to stay strong and carry on. The experience also made him realise that given enough time, alcohol always amplifies every pain, anxiety and hopeless thought. This was the main reason he'd given it up all those years ago. Thank God he returned to being the calm, objective man that I have come to depend on and never went back to alcohol.

CHAPTER 25

More Proof the Private Equity Firms Play Dirty

Soon after "Dragons' Den" (known as "Shark Tank" in the US) in 2009, I was approached by an agent. He contacted me while I was in business with James Caan and Duncan Bannatyne, two of the investors on the programme. During one of my trips to London this agent introduced me to a lawyer called Dean.

When things didn't work out with James, Dean became my lifeline. He reviewed my business contract and said it was one of the worst he'd ever seen. He also attended the final meeting with James after I'd made the choice to break our partnership agreement.

My last book "Mother of Invention" details the intimidation I was subjected to. Looking back now I wonder if my exit had been pre-planned, or was it because I am constantly in fight or flight mode and questioning my past through the same suspicious lens.

The reason it has taken me so long to come to terms with my "Dragons' Den" experience was because James never took any accountability for his wrongdoings. I have also never fully explained what had happened after I took legal action. My lawyer informed me that he was beaten up by Caan's thugs who ordered him to drop my lawsuit against him.

All these years I've lived with this information, fearful of what would happen if I exposed James Caan's mafia-style tactics. I chose not to say anything back then, but I was wrong not to speak up. Living in fear is a form of psychological control that no human being should be subjected to.

So now I am going to tell the world about the assault I was informed of and do not care about being sued for defamation of character because I believe what I'm saying is the truth and Dean will bear witness to that.

In 2009 I sued James Caan and the case was due to be heard in the High Court in London. Dean was training to be a barrister at the time (and is currently training to be a judge.) The trial date was set, but a few days later I received a message that James Caan had to cancel "due to unforeseen circumstances." This was despite being seen in The Ivy in London that day by a friend of his. I believe he said he had to take an emergency trip overseas.

This made me so angry. It was a dirty tactic to push back on the court hearing after we were all psyched up and ready to go. A second date was agreed and in order to prepare myself for this stressful event I decided to take a holiday to calm my mind. I relaxed in the sun, ate healthily and reached a certain level of peace.

One day I returned to my hotel room and saw I'd missed a call from Dean. He knew I was on holiday. The case was well prepared so I didn't understand why he needed to talk to me. He knew that if I was offered money to drop the case I would refuse. I was determined that nobody else should go through the same ordeal as me and for James Caan to take accountability.

My heart was racing. I had this horrible gut feeling that something was wrong. Dean sounded so flat and tired. He told me, "I was invited to an office block in London to discuss the lawsuit. When I arrived the office was empty except for two hard looking men who beat me up quite badly. They demanded the lawsuit against Caan was dropped and told me to make it go away." I only have Dean's word for this, but I have no reason to disbelieve him.

At this point I felt my heart would collapse it was beating so hard. I had been a victim of Caan's intimidation and felt strongly defensive of Dean. I felt so bad that he had to experience such a horrendous event and strongly urged him to go to the police.

Dean said he couldn't because the hitmen were sitting in their car outside his house and he had to think of his children. I didn't know how to respond. I didn't want to appear selfish, but I remember saying, "But you're my lawyer and you have a duty of care. If they can do this to you, what will they do to me? We need protection from the police."

I could hear the defeat in his voice. He couldn't expose his family to the possibility of getting hurt or risk his life further. At this point I was crying. I told him that as soon as I returned to the UK, I would contact him.

I had three days left of my holiday during which time I analysed my options. I was sure that when Dean got over the shock, he would report the matter to the police. He had taken the bar exam and had to tell the truth. This was gangster-style movie drama that didn't happen in real life!

I spoke with a good friend of mine called Colin who I'd met earlier that year while on holiday in Dubai. Colin and his wife Marianne had been sitting opposite me at the pool. By the strangest coincidence they were both reading a copy of "Mother of Invention."

I went up to them to make sure it really was my book and introduced myself. It was a bizarre situation and I remember feeling a sense of pride and excitement from the recognition. I knew I had sold a lot of books, but I did not expect to see my face on the cover and the words I'd written being read out here in Dubai.

I have since kept in touch with this couple and have visited their beautiful home on several occasions. In fact, we all went on holiday to Barbados together the following year. Colin understood my journey and felt very protective of me and for that I will always be grateful. He related to being fucked over because the same thing had happened to him. Business attracts many people to the party. A lot of them just cling on to your coat tails to see what benefits they can get out of you.

Colin's advice was to enjoy the rest of my holiday and speak to Dean when I was back in the UK. He also advised me to record the conversation for my own protection. He wondered if maybe Dean had been bought off. Could he have been promised future legal business from James. Or was he just scared? Colin was right to question the situation.

I left Dean to calm down and think things through. One thing he wouldn't be expecting was for me to travel to London to see him unannounced. As soon as my holiday ended, I went straight down to London. I was shown into Dean's office and sat down opposite him at his desk. There were no bruises on his face or hands, so I asked him why he had no visible marks or cuts. He indicated with his hand to the area of his stomach. He could see I was sceptical, so he stood up and said, "Come on, let's grab a coffee."

We went down the road to a café where he bought us both a coffee and we sat outside so I could smoke a cigarette. I had a large bag that I could leave open which had my phone inside. I pressed record and carefully placed it near the top of the bag.

Dean proceeded to tell me about his ordeal again. I can tell when someone is telling the truth by their mannerisms. After he'd finished, I was only 50% convinced the attack had happened. The lack of evidence of any physical damage was my main issue.

I wanted him so badly to tell the police the same story, but he convinced me to let it go. Then he said that if I continued with the court case, I had to seriously consider the risk that I could lose my house. What? Up until this point he'd told me I had a very good chance of winning!

I went to Colin's house, played him the recording and we talked about the possible ways to go forward. I made the decision to forget the lawsuit and move on. Then I went on the sell my Magnamole business with Dean handling all the legal work. Afterwards we had very little contact.

In 2019 he called me to say he'd been approached by someone in the USA who wanted to know about the tooling on my product and the patent. For some reason they contacted him instead of me. It's only now writing this book I wonder what that conversation was really all about. What I do remember was that when Dean called me it came from a withheld number so the only way I could contact him was through his old email address.

With Commercide's lawsuit against myself and John, I have been limited as far as legal help due to a lack of funds because I have been prevented from releasing equity from my house. But I have spoken to three independent solicitors and two barristers regarding the litigation. They all say Commercide will struggle to win the case against us after seeing the evidence. Furthermore, they have nothing to back up their accusations.

I spoke to Dean about representing us, but he had to refuse due to other work commitments and also because he was about to become a judge. Then in February 2023 I sent him an email and he called me back. God must have been shining down on me that day because my iPad recorded him admitting that he was beaten up by thugs who'd been sent by James Caan from "Dragon's Den."

I had been approached by yet another "truth teller" on TikTok and because he spoke so fast, I had to record what he was saying. I had set my iPad to record, when Dean called half way through our conversation. I hung up on the TikTok guy to speak to Dean and didn't realise I'd recorded him until afterwards.

(Incidentally, the "truth teller" was another bullshitter. He claimed to have set up a finance company, but it was a company John had previously worked with. A quick check confirmed he'd never had anything to do with it.)

I wanted Dean to tell the truth about James Caan as it was another example of the tactics used by the corporate bullies, so I sent him this email:

"Hi Dean, I am asking you to tell the truth. This is cruel mental torture and I will not just accept any of this. I have had threats on my life and that is unforgivable. I am asking you to tell the truth so that people can be held accountable."

"I have no idea what you are talking about? What are you asking me? Who has threatened you?" he replied.

"You should tell the truth about James Caan beating you up. They used the same tactics as Commercide. They took advantage of me knowing my mental health issues and they expected me to take my life. That's a threat to me when they use my vulnerability to their advantage. If you tell the truth about what James Caan did to you people would listen to me. I am just being ignored and my voice doesn't count. It's wrong."

Later that day he said, "Actually I have an idea how to get this out in the open. I'll explore it over the next few days and talk it over with you next week."

He called me to say he'd speak to the all-party Parliamentary Group which is composed of members of parliament. With their help you can make changes to the law to get private equity firms regulated. I am still waiting to hear back from him about this and will admit, I'm not holding my breath.

He has since lost his brother in a car accident, following which his sister-in-law took her own life. This has understandably affected him massively. Each time I've spoken to him he has sounded very depressed, so I have to be respectful of the situation he's in.

John and I have been so disappointed by the way people have reacted to our situation. One of John's friends is still working at Buildadeck. He was told not to talk to us or discuss the court case or deal with us at any level while we were in litigation. He even suggested that we should give Buildadeck a few hundred thousand pounds so the lawsuit against us would be dropped.

I visited "The Lawns Show" the same year we were fired to help a friend with her furniture business and noticed people were avoiding me. A few of them asked odd questions like, "Why did you leave?" We have since heard a number of stories from ex-employees at Buildadeck that Commercide told them the staff had paid for our house to be built.

They were also told that once there was a pot of gold for driving the business forward, but that pot of gold had been stolen." Commercide's nasty slurs on our character have caused us both great distress and will be addressed in our legal action when we sue them for defamation of character.

People have said, "Let it go. Move on and get your life back." But when we ask them if they were really in the same position at the age we are and had gone through all this stress could they walk away and let the cheats and liars win? Not one of them could answer that question. We haven't listened to what other people think of us because none of them has walked in our shoes. They haven't been professionally shafted twice or are at risk of losing their home.

I keep remembering the recorded conversation we had between ourselves and Nick when he told us, "You will spend the rest of your days fighting litigation." To him, business is all about breaking people down. It's all about crushing the "little people" with less money and power. If everyone gives in to them, they're giving them a green light to continue their reign of terror. My total disgust at their blatant manipulation and coercion incentivises me to keep going.

Nick also said we would run out of money. We may not have the finances to defend ourselves but we have the evidence to show we are not guilty of what we have been accused of. Telling the truth costs nothing. Even if it means we have to live on one Pot Noodle a day and rob Peter to pay Paul (I really should change that name to Simon!) we will make sure we have our day in court.

It beggars belief how many unscrupulous private equity firms there are and they need to be stopped. They promise they want to realise the company's potential, but all they want is to fatten it up and offload it as quickly as possible for fast money.

These predatory operations are run by callous, exploitative people who have no qualms about stealing from trusting entrepreneurs and hard-working business owners who think they are dealing with genuine investors. Not only do these equity firms destroy them, they terrorise them and drag them through legal quagmires to financially and emotionally ruin them. In reality, it's these sociopathic parasites who should have their assets seized because they are basically the proceeds of crime.

On 4 December 2024 we applied for a motion to strike out and a court date was set for March 5th 2025. The purpose of a motion to strike is to address issues like scandalous or frivolous statements. In our case it's Commercide's false allegations with zero evidence to support them.

After hearing arguments from both sides and considering all the facts a judge then decides whether to grant the motion to strike. If

Commercide's lawsuit is struck out it would mean the freezing order on the house would be lifted and Nick would have no reason to continue his legal action. It's a high-risk strategy, but far quicker than having to wait years for our case to be heard.

Nick has seen our responses to all his false accusations. He has been provided with all the evidence to prove we never stole from our company or committed fraud. This is even before we provide full disclosure. We have also forwarded him emails that were sent between him and us in case he has deleted evidence or denies knowledge of approving our request to buy building materials through the company and offsetting the costs against monies I was owed.

I believe all private equity firms do in-depth due diligence on the individuals they invest in and look for people with previous legal issues or mental health problems because these are weaknesses they can weaponise. Kindness, honesty, diligence and an obsessive work ethic are also qualities that can be exploited by the avaricious psychopaths of this world.

They examine your Facebook page, delve into your background records and arm themselves with as much ammunition against you as they can find. John losing his Safestyle case and conflict with James Caan made us prime targets. Because we'd already been through hell fighting for money we were rightfully owed in the past, Commercide probably thought we wouldn't have the stomach to defend ourselves in court.

I now think it was God's plan to have John and I expose this injustice. John has the brains and is like a silent assassin the way he collects documented evidence. And I have the tenacity to fight against theft and corruption and will not be intimidated by bully boy tactics. Neither of us will rest until there is legislation to ensure these predators are not only brought to task, but no investment firm is allowed to operate like this in the future.

CAPITAL PUNISHMENT

CHAPTER 26

An Intruder Comes to the House

On Christmas Day John went to collect his children from Leeds so they could spend a few days with us while I stayed home and cooked dinner. He left the house at 1:00pm. At 1:30pm there was a man in our garden videoing the inside of our house. I could see him on the CCTV cameras.

He was dressed all in black with a cap on his head and looked like he had ginger hair. He had come through the next door's garden and into ours. We are on a private road at the far side of the village set in grounds of around two acres. There is no reason to come onto our property as it is not a shortcut to anything.

I was upstairs in the bedroom and watched as he walked straight across our lawn, took a camera from his pocket and started taking photos through the picture windows at the back of our house. I stepped out onto the balcony and shouted down to him, "Hello! Can I help you?"

He replied, "Sorry I was just passing by and thought the house was empty."

On Christmas Day? He could clearly see our house was fully furnished. Yet he had no qualms about standing there for nearly three minutes dressed like a cat burglar. Wow! Maybe he had been sent to intimidate me! His arrival had been timed to coincide with

John's departure when I was alone. Was his appearance related to my text to Nick?

I watched as he walked back to his car and could just see the road he was parked on. I called my neighbours Sarah and Steve. In the past they couldn't do enough to welcome us into the village but something had changed. She didn't return my call until much later.

The next day I said to John, "I won't live in fear anymore. I refuse to let intimidation haunt me if that's what this is. I'm going to post a Facebook message asking if any of our neighbours have CCTV cameras and see if we can identify this man or the van he was driving."

To my horror the next day a neighbour posted a photo of a man with a bald head and ginger hair with the words, "WARNING! Everyone in and around Brigg please stay alert this festive season. A man named Nick Jones (41) is reportedly going door to door pretending to need help, only to attack innocent people. Last Friday, he brutally assaulted a single mother with a knife, leaving her fighting for her life. He has also been accused of stealing a car from an 84-year-old woman after offering to help her unload groceries. This man is armed and dangerous. If you see him, do NOT engage. Call the authorities immediately. Spread the word and keep your loved ones informed. Stay safe."

I called the police to tell them about my encounter with this individual and to confirm if the threat was real. Two police officers arrived. One of them said, "This is not the first time something like this has happened to you, is it?"

The said they couldn't comment on the Facebook post but they would look into it. We were given a crime number but of course we heard nothing after that.

CAPITAL PUNISHMENT

CHAPTER 27

My Strange Medical Drama

My dad was now 80. Since mum died in 2021, he hadn't really moved out of his chair in his front room. He had also lost his beloved dog Ollie a few years after mum. He'd seen a lot, heard a lot and was desperately worried for me and the trials I faced.

It was almost like I was a magnet for drama. Was it because I had been in the wrong place at the wrong time, or was it divine planning? Had I been sent to this earth to wake people up? I have never really enjoyed life and believe my destiny was perfectly timed to write this book and tell people what is going on and how the super-elite are stealing everything they can with no regard for human life, except theirs.

A few days before the Christmas of 2024, the doctors' surgery called to tell me some recent blood tests showed something concerning and they needed me to come in and have more tests done as soon as I could. When I asked the receptionist what they had seen of course she didn't know, but she said a doctor would call me later that day.

I couldn't believe the rude and arrogant way he spoke to me! When I asked why I needed my blood tests to be repeated he wouldn't tell me. He just said, "When they are done again, we'll let you know."

This was just going to play on my mind all Christmas, so I pushed him a little harder saying he must have an idea what the testing is

CAPITAL PUNISHMENT

for. Eventually he told me my red blood count and my lymph results showed some irregularities. I asked him what that meant. Was it diabetes or cancer? He snapped at me, "I never said it was cancer!"

I pushed him again and said, "If you are testing me again you must at least know what you are looking for." Annoyingly he gave the same response. I was so shocked I burst into tears. All I wanted was a peaceful Christmas and this doctor wasn't going to tell me what they thought was wrong with me until next week. I put the phone down and calmed myself down, determined not to let this spoil the holiday.

Then dad called me. He was beside himself with worry, saying a doctor had just called him to pass a message to me to say I needed to go in for important blood tests straight after Christmas. I was fuming that this man had upset my dad. Plus, I thought my information and messages were supposed to be private.

After reassuring him I was fine, I called the surgery to ask if all their calls were recorded. The receptionist assured me they were. So I said, "Go back and listen to the conversation I just had with the doctor and ask why he was allowed to call my dad." The receptionist looked on the system and said my dad was listed as my next of kin.

I said, "That's rubbish! I left home 33 years ago and have had two husbands in that time. He hasn't been my next of kin for years!"

Then I realised the only person getting stressed with what was going on was me. I needed to change my response. If this was orchestrated in some way, I couldn't let it get to me.

Regardless of the risks of not getting the tests redone I have ignored all their requests to get more tests done. I know you probably think I'm a crazy conspiracy theorist, but I'm too terrified to go to any doctor or health care professional now.

The doctor's office has left me many messages saying I need to go in for more blood tests but how could I trust any of them? Once again, I remembered Paul the Freemason's warning, "They are in the medical profession too…"

CAPITAL PUNISHMENT

CHAPTER 28

Our House is Featured in the Daily Mail

As we were unable to reach a compromise with the architects, we had no option to file a lawsuit against them in the High Court in Leeds. They had strung us along for many months to delay us from taking legal action by making us think they would agree to a settlement. The filing was done electronically so we didn't need to go to the courthouse.

Imagine our shock when we returned home that day to find a reporter outside our house. He leapt out of his car when he saw us and said he'd been waiting for us for several hours. He wanted to write a news article about our legal action.

My hackles were raised. I asked him "why?" He said he recognised my name (which was bullshit) and that I was a bit famous. I immediately panicked and replied, "No. I am not interested in doing a story." John turned to me and said, "I thought you wanted a voice. Now is your perfect opportunity."

The reporter then said, "Well I'm writing about it anyway and we've already approached the architect's solicitors for their comments." Now I was angry. So they were happy to respond immediately with their opinions but were denying our claim against them and refusing to talk to us?

I agreed to tell my side of the story on the condition that I wrote it down. When we got inside the house this guy's beady eyes were darting everywhere to work out what kind of photos he would take. He didn't stay long. He took one shot of us on the stairs and a couple of the unfinished parts of the house. What I didn't know was he'd already taken shots of the exterior and was going to write his piece with or without my written contribution.

He agreed to let me write a piece for him to edit. I insisted that I didn't want to bad mouth Declan even though he'd refused to take accountability for all his mistakes. I blamed all the delays on reaching an agreement with his insurance company.

A lot of time had passed and Declan had no doubt reflected on his company's wrongdoings. In my opinion he had taken his eye off the ball. Our house design had been delegated to many people within his group but since the lockdown they all worked from home. In my opinion, this meant there was a lack of coordination and a risk that errors would be missed.

That night I wrote the piece and sent it to the reporter who later passed it on to the Mail Online. I wrote it very respectfully, because despite everything I couldn't live with myself if his business was affected or he did something stupid. That's the empath in me. Not one person would have done the same thing for me and I know that.

In the early hours of the morning, I woke up with a jolt. It suddenly hit me. The timing of the reporter arriving was suspicious. He arrived the week before we were having a survey done on the house to determine how much it was worth. I knew in my heart that this was one big set up so the house could be devalued.

I immediately messaged the reporter to say I'd changed my mind and didn't want to go ahead with the article. He replied that it had

CAPITAL PUNISHMENT

already been passed on to the papers and the only way to stop it being published was to contact them all.

I emailed and called the Daily Mail and eventually got through to one of their editors. He said I would need a very good reason to stop the story from being released. I explained that I had recently attempted to take my life and was not in the right frame of mind to deal with all the publicity. To my horror they went ahead and printed the story online. Thankfully it was only visible for a few hours.

There were around 20 comments. One of them was from a supposed friend of mine called Tom. Here are some examples of the nasty backlash we received:

"Amble Architecture is going to lose customers. What a nightmare this couple has caused"

"Looks like Sharon and husband have no idea about managing a project"

"As always blame someone else... she seems to slander everyone involved. None of it is their fault according to them. I do like modern architecture... but that looks like a JW church I'm afraid"

"And it's giving her a neck problem. Or she is one of those tilty head selfie idiots"

"I assume the £625 grand house that was already there wasn't ugly enough"

"It all sounds absolutely dreadful"

"The woman has ADHD. That fact shouldn't be ignored. It means she could have changed her mind a million times and was speaking at 100 miles an hour so the contactors struggled to follow anything she was saying"

"She's hardly a star of the show. She had fifteen minutes of fame many years ago"

"Dragons Den star? Who is she?"

Tom informed me the next day that he was the one who commented that it all sounds absolutely dreadful. There was another one in there that was really disgusting and mentioned John's disability and it eventually got removed. All the comments were clearly meant to upset me.

What I find insulting is the people who set out to create this negative publicity about John and I would think we were too stupid to realise what they had done. I knew very well that the purpose of the article was to knock hundreds of thousands off the value of the property.

The surveyor was a very good friend of the people who were thinking of buying the house. I remember them telling me this when we first met. They also mentioned that either his or her dad was a solicitor. This surveyor had obviously done many valuations for them in the past.

Then it struck me that I had foolishly given a key to my house to my friends Tom and Susan whose daughter owned a restaurant with a pub in the village. I'd also given them a copy of all my information on a memory stick and asked them to keep it safe.

Then I remembered the people who had initially offered £2.2 million and then reduced their offer to £1.5 million. It suddenly dawned on me. They must know Tom and Susan because they'd mentioned that they drank in their pub all the time. Omg! I jumped in my car to retrieve my key from Tom. I was so naïve! Why hadn't I seen the connection?

Whenever I got news about our legal cases, or spoke to MPs and the police, in fact everything that was happening to us, Tom and Susan were the first people I'd told. Whether it was good nor bad news they were always keen to hear the updates. I realised they were spies in the camp.

Tom was shocked when I told him I wanted my key back. I made an excuse saying I needed to get another one cut and would give it back to him later. I didn't want to spook him because I didn't want him to know I'd sussed him out. So I continued to visit Tom and Susan for a few more weeks to confirm my suspicions.

What gave them away was the survey. I'd told Tom about some very small niggles I noticed with the house, and bizarrely these barely noticeable faults were highlighted in the report as quite serious concerns.

I'd given Tom a memory stick detailing everything that was happening with Commercide and Amble Architecture as well as other personal information for safekeeping in case anything happened to me. So, I called him and said I needed to update the material because so much more had happened since I'd given him my files. He denied having received it!

I told him I remembered clearly exactly who I'd given copies to and he was one of them. How could he deny it? Did he want me to think I was going crazy? We all know the answer to that.

A week or so before our court date to ask to strike out Commercide's lawsuit against us, Susan sent me a text to ask if I was okay and if I wanted to come over for a coffee. No doubt it was to check on me and see how I was bearing up. I told her I was fine and just busy. A few days later I sent her the following message:

"I have to get this off my chest in order to move on. You took my kindness for weakness and then you rubbed salt in. I suspected Tom was friends with the potential house buyers but I hoped I was wrong. I do not need friends like you and this is me setting my boundaries."

The response notification showed that she had read my message immediately. Exactly an hour later she replied with, "Sharon, I really have no idea what you mean. Neither Tom or I know the buyers. I value you as a friend and always have since we first met and I would do anything to help you. I have not bothered you recently as I felt you were wanting your own space.

I will always be here for you. I have always valued your kindness and I hoped you valued mine. I've missed you in the last few weeks but have been having a few problems here. I hope your boundaries still include me as I have always believed in you and your strength to go through all the shit you are dealing with. If you and John ever need me, I am always here x."

I cried. Was it me going crazy? I sent her a text apologising, but then I had time to feel what my gut was telling me. I was sure I was right. These two were relaying everything I said to my adversaries.

After that I received a message on the day of our court appearance wishing us well and a couple more saying she missed me, I ignored them. As far as I was concerned, I didn't need to explain anything to them anymore.

Then out of the blue I received a call from my good friend called Marcus, who I hadn't heard from in months. I had figured him out too and was keeping him at arms-length. He had been the first one to mention the Freemasons and had then proceeded to humour me about my TV show idea. After that he'd kept his distance. I decided to let him keep thinking I was a fool and easily manipulated. Maybe he was calling to assess my frame of mind before the court hearing.

Curious as to what he wanted to say. He seemed nervous, like he had something to get off his chest. He said he was just checking in to make sure that me and him were okay. I asked, "Why wouldn't we be?"

He mumbled that he had been suffering and had been off work with a few health problems. I said I was sorry to hear that and hoped he recovered soon.

Shortly after this I asked a good friend of mine to record another video in case I didn't get to speak out in court or Commercide somehow managed to convince people their claims against us were valid.

I must have talked for around two hours but never mentioned the names Buildadeck or Commercide. I mentioned all the coercion, manipulation and bullying I'd suffered over the previous two years and that I could prove every statement that came out of my mouth.

The video was edited down to 48 minutes. My friend worked at speed to put it all together and he did an amazing, professional job. I uploaded it onto YouTube on LinkedIn, Facebook and TikTok. I also sent copies to Trump, Vance, Kennedy, Tiffany and our government.

Usually when I post a video it gets a massive response. My first TikTok video had over half a million views, most of which came within the first 24 hours. I expected the same with this one. Disappointingly, the video got less than a thousand views on TikTok.

It was the same on the other platforms. Barely anyone clicked on it. As I suspected when I looked at the data for my post the key words to find me had been removed. I'd been shadow banned and my voice had been silenced. Commercide's lawyers had got to them.

Despite the limited audience I was contacted by a TikTok friend who had been through something similar, so we face timed each other privately. I sympathised as he sat in his car and cried and warned me not to lose everything in court like he had.

I told this guy that I wouldn't lose my house. Nobody could take it from me and with respect, I wasn't him. I wouldn't hide in fear or stay silent. I knew God was protecting me and the truth always comes out in the end. The only way they could stop me telling the truth of all the injustices they had dumped on me now was to kill me.

He went on to tell me he had lost everything and had ended up in a rented house living a simple life and was far happier. At that moment I switched off. I had done nothing wrong. He didn't know the exact details of my circumstances, so how could he sit there and give me advice and compare himself to me? I wasn't rude, but I made sure I said everything I wanted to say to whoever had sent him.

This time the James Caan-style threats and scare tactics wouldn't work on me. Whatever school these idiots went to for lessons on how to be intimidating it wasn't working anymore. That's because the fear in me has completely gone.

Even if there is a lion outside the courtroom doors, I'll just push it out of the way now. Nothing is going to stop me getting the truth out there and telling my story.

CAPITAL PUNISHMENT

CHAPTER 29

Rita Reminds Me She Bought Sunflowers Not Daffodils

My good friend Rita asked if she could take John and I out for Sunday lunch. We've both been financially successful and usually pay for everyone else, so her offer came as something of a pleasant surprise.

To be honest, I have sometimes spent money on other people because it was in my interest. For example, I've paid for people to come on holiday with me rather than go by myself. But if someone was struggling, I'd always go out of my way to support them. John is a bit tighter with his money, maybe because he's a true Yorkshireman.

Back in the days of my invention I had no choice but to travel solo because money was tight. I'd often gone on holidays alone, but these days my confidence was shot. Whenever I had needed a break, it wasn't always at the same time as John which was also a problem. He either couldn't or wouldn't go on holiday with me, saying he was too busy at work, so I had taken friends instead, Rita being one of them.

Rita and I had an amazing week in Egypt and I never expected anything in return other than her friendship. She was so appreciative that I had done something so generous and wanted to reciprocate in her own modest way.

During the lunch she talked about a video I'd recently uploaded talking about all the strange things that had been going on in my life. She was confused as to why I said the flowers she bought me were daffodils and not sunflowers. She went on to emphasise that she always gives sunflowers because it was her favourite flower and seemed annoyed that I could make such a silly mistake.

I told her that all I remembered was that they were yellow flowers. It wasn't really important to me what kind of flowers they were. I just remembered the event. I found it odd she would take offence at such a petty thing. Then she asked about our preparations for our court hearing the following week. Again, she seemed irritated when we told her we felt positive and were well prepared.

After a bit of an awkward silence, she mentioned that she had bumped into our neighbours Sarah and Steve the previous week at a local pub and told us Sarah had been bitching about me. Apparently, she had been telling everyone I was saying some crazy stuff about a Freemason man. Rita said she had defended me and said she had seen the evidence for herself.

I was shocked that Sarah had said all that. Rita told me not to mention anything to Sarah and I assured her I wouldn't. Sarah and Steve hadn't spoken to us for months. We had lost all of our so-called friends, probably because they were scared of what was happening to us and thought we were tied up in some kind of gangster warfare.

My suspicions about Sarah were raised when she called me after seeing the post on Facebook about the dangerous man patrolling the village at Christmas. When I told her I'd seen him outside our property she said, "I'd be shitting myself if I was you. Are you not scared?" It was like she was deliberately reminding me I should feel isolated and vulnerable. It was all disgusting. I didn't need people like that in my life.

A few days after our lunch with Rita I posted another TikTok video about recovering from trauma. I told everyone that God wouldn't send us into a situation unless there was a lesson to be learned. Rita called me and went ballistic because I'd mentioned religion. She raged, "There is no God! If there was, he wouldn't take children at a young age or give them horrible illnesses."

I was shocked that she was trying to impose her beliefs on me. It's a personal choice if someone wants to believe in God. Plus, it was my TikTok platform and I had the right to say whatever I wanted. I wasn't ramming my beliefs down anyone's throats. So, the fact she was pushing hers onto me was hypocritical.

I came off the call and considered how angry she'd been. Rita is very opinionated like me. She'd had a hard life too and I admired her strength and tenacity. Then I sat and thought about our friendship for a moment and the subject of the sunflowers preyed on my mind.

OMG! I was so naive! Why am I always late to the party? Rita was friends with Marcus who was a Freemason.

Paul the Freemason "healer" had moved the flowers in front of the camera the same day that Rita had given them to me. The penny dropped. I wasn't being watched. All these seemingly innocuous "coincidences" had been planned in an attempt to mess with my head. No wonder she had distanced herself from us after he'd been to our house. She was scared that we would realise what was going on.

We had built up what I thought was a real friendship, but if my suspicions were correct – and the evidence was mounting that I was – Rita was in on some sadistic group game to make me feel and look as if I was losing my mind. Another little clue something was going on was that John had seen Sarah's husband in the village a few weeks later and he had deliberately turned the other way while walking his dog to avoid acknowledging him.

Rather than react, I made the decision at that point to avoid Rita too. So much for our friendship and everything I had done for her. I had no idea there was so much simmering jealousy around me and that so many people wanted to break me down.

Shortly after I cut Rita out of my life, she announced on Facebook that her brother had passed away. Although I didn't want to interact with her, what sort of person would I be if I didn't say something? I called and she seemed quite happy when she answered. I told her I was sorry to hear the sad news to which she replied, "That's okay. He brought it on himself with his drinking and we didn't particularly get on anyway."

Wow! You can still love someone without liking their actions, especially your own brother! I made the call short and sweet. Now there was no need to speak to her again.

Then all the pennies dropped at once. Gerry, Marcus, Susan, Tom and Rita were all in it together! I couldn't be sure that this was really the case, but my suspicions were usually correct. I just needed clear evidence to finally prove to myself what was going on.

CAPITAL PUNISHMENT

The day before our court hearing for our motion to strike out, my dad called. We usually speak every day and see each other once or twice a week. As it was early morning, I knew something was wrong. He'd been poorly for over three days with diarrhoea and was vomiting quite badly. We'd both thought he had a stomach bug and would recover.

He said he needed help and asked if I could call his doctor and arrange for him to visit. I got through to the doctors' surgery, but they don't do home visits anymore. They advised me to take him to the A & E. My dad is terrified of hospitals after he was stuck in one for months with a heart infection and after his recent fall.

The previous year he'd woken up early in the morning and was desperate to get to the loo, but his foot had got tangled in his quilt. He lost his balance and fell head first into his TV and broke his neck in three places at the top of his spine and had to wear a halo neck support for months. Nurses visited him morning and night and helped him dress and shower. He didn't have much luck. When he did something, he really did it good and proper!

Dad's fear of hospitals was understandable and awful to watch. I felt helpless and selfish but I had waited for this court date for years and I didn't dare risk catching what we believed to be norovirus. So, it was agreed my older brother Dean would take him to hospital this time. The guilt I felt that day unsettled me. Why did saying "no" to something I couldn't do put so much pressure on me?

The hospital believed he'd acquired an infection and suspected he had sepsis. I couldn't risk not seeing him, especially after what happened to mum. So I took the risk and went to visit him. In my head I was saying my goodbyes. It was yet another worry I had to bear the day before our court hearing.

On the morning of the hearing Rita and Susan both sent texts wishing me luck. No doubt they were annoyed and surprised that I was ignoring them both. To me they were just vultures perched high up on a tree branch eyeing up their prey from afar.

CHAPTER 30

Gerry Shows His True Colours

Gerry turned out to be another member of the gang of backstabbers I once believed were my friends. He used to hang out with my brother Gary when they were schoolkids and we'd stayed in touch for years. He was a plumber by trade and had done quite well for himself and his wife was a well-respected teacher.

They decided to move to Australia a few years ago to live in the sunshine and enjoy a better quality of life. Unfortunately, it didn't work out for them, so they'd returned to England. Because of all the upheavals, disappointments and blows to his pride, Gerry suffered a bad breakdown. The next we heard, he'd tried to take his own life and had spent a long time in Great Oakes, a free in-patient facility, trying to rebuild his mental health.

After he left the facility, a local businessman called Derek saw that he was still struggling and offered to help him get back on his feet and rejoin the community. Scunthorpe is a small town and everyone knows everyone.

Derek had owned a men's clothing shop for many years and was always campaigning to save the town centre where his shop was located. His business was struggling and he was frustrated and angry at the way Scunthorpe had degenerated. Stores had shut down due mainly to the effects of online shopping.

High rents, high parking costs and the inconvenience of getting there had also contributed to the huge drop in customers and boarded up shop fronts. Now the centre looked shabby, deserted and run-down, making it even less appealing. The only people who hung around the place were homeless drug addicts and drunks, who congregated in its empty pedestrian walkways because there was safety in numbers.

Derek socialised with my ex-husband, so of course I knew him too, but I was still a little surprised to hear from him when randomly called me for a general chit chat. I sensed he was nervous at the beginning. Then he suddenly surprised me by saying. "Listen Sharon, I have a favour to ask you."

Immediately I knew it was about money. He asked me if I could lend him £5,000. I'll help anyone who will help themselves, but £5,000 was a lot to ask, especially as we weren't that close. I also knew he'd have difficulties returning it because I was aware his business was struggling. I asked what the money was for to get a better idea of his situation and suggest other ways to help.

He told me he needed it for Christmas presents for his two grandchildren. At that point I thought, "No way, was I spending that kind of money on mine!" I offered to take him shopping to buy whatever presents he needed and I'd pay for them. He didn't need to return the money. It was a gift. He seemed grateful for the offer but he politely declined it.

A few months later Derek called to tell me that he and Gerry had set up a support group for men who were suffering mental health problems. He told me they had benefited from supporting each other and wanted to give other men the same opportunity. They were using a local hotel for their weekly meetings where tea, coffee and snacks were provided.

He told me it cost £200 to hire a conference room at The Wortley House Hotel. I thought their efforts were amazing and could see that Derek's request for money had a purpose. So, I cleared it with John and Paul and said I'd give him £1,000 through the business as a charitable donation. The money was transferred into their bank account.

Not long after, Derek called again. He knew I'd done a lot of after dinner speaking in the past which had generated revenue for the event's host. He asked if I'd consider speaking at a breakfast meeting for local businesses and encourage others to donate to the cause. I was happy to accommodate in any way that I could so I agreed.

On the morning of the event, I discovered Derek had attracted a lot of attention from the local business community. I also noticed that Derek had also invited Marcus, Rita and Gerry as they were all very good friends.

I gave my presentation and encouraged others to contribute to this good cause. Then I went to the bar to get a drink. I knew the owner of the hotel from when we had worked together in the past. What he told me completely changed my opinion of Derek.

The hotel owner explained that he'd done his bit for Derek's cause by donating the room and providing all the refreshments for free. Derek had lied to me about the cost of the room hire! I left the event feeling angry and used and vowed never to support them again. For a while I felt really guilty. My reputation was at stake and I had duped all these business people into lining Derek's pockets. But it wasn't my place to say anything so I let it go.

I watched on Facebook as his group continued to rake in donations by organising numerous charity events. SAS Paul would regularly speak at their events. When local people lost their loved ones, the families of the deceased would raise money for the mental health group. They seemed to be flying!

Then rumours started spreading around the town. Derek was raising a lot of money but nobody could see what it was being spent on. People were getting angry. Marcus told me he had left the group after a disagreement with Derek about making the accounts public.

To everyone's surprise, Derek then announced he was opening a new shop. Someone had previously checked him out on Companies House and it was obvious he was trying to hide his past. With each new venture he would enter a slightly different date of birth. Sometimes he would have a middle name and sometimes he wouldn't.

I was fuming because it looked suspicious as to where all the money had gone. I couldn't resist going on Facebook and asking how he could afford to set up in business when a few months earlier he was so desperate for funds.

I received a huge number of replies. Half of them support me for having the courage to ask what people were thinking. The other half were furious that I had asked the question and sent the most insulting messages. Gerry was especially angry and viciously attacked me online. I later went on to regret speaking out on behalf of everyone else.

After being accused of being a conman, Derek attempted to take his life. His support group continued for a while, but without Derek the momentum had gone.

Out of the blue a few months later, Gerry contacted me to apologise and said I'd been right all along. Derek had used him to help him generate funds to set himself up in another business. But despite this conciliatory message it seems Gerry (and his daughter), Marcus, Rita and SAS Paul never forgave me for exposing Derek's scam. Given all their efforts to break me, it would appear they plotted their revenge.

CAPITAL PUNISHMENT

CHAPTER 31

The Pressure is Too Much for John

I never expected the judge to dismiss Commercide's claims against us. It's far easier to prove your innocence when you can present all the documents and provide clear evidence that proves your case. Despite my scepticism we submitted our application for a strike out and hoped for the best.

Unfortunately, since Covid, the courts are many months behind for things like this and other legal matters that seriously impact your finances and your life. I know the difference between criminal and civil law and that our issues are all civil but the principles are the same,

As with a lot of things these days there seems to be a two-tier system where certain issues are more important than others. For example, if you post opinions on social media that alarm the government or the "fact checkers" you are in a cell within hours and in court within days. Did you know the UK is arresting 30 people a day for "thought crimes?"

On the other hand, if you are personally subjected to psychological lawfare and your future is at stake, you are dumped into an administrative maze that makes it virtually impossible to get a confirmed court date. There are so many hoops to get through.

If you don't have the funds to pay for a lawyer to deal with all the obstacles and obtain the information you need, the claimant's legal team will just play ping pong with you. In view of all these complexities, the simplest option for us was to go for a strike out which involves a maximum of a day's hearing.

A month before the hearing for our application for a strike out, on February 20th 2025, I'd woken John up in the early hours. I'd received what I call a "spiritual download" and knew Buildadeck had filed something at Companies House. John checked the site and there it was, in black and white, Commercide was no longer involved with Buildadeck. Nick and all bar one of his associates had withdrawn from the company altogether. This was exactly what Tiffany had warned me might happen.

Buildadeck hadn't filed their accounts for 30 months. The fact they had avoided doing so spoke volumes. I had wanted the judge to make Commercide Ventures commit to the security of funds should they be ordered to pay us damages, but now because they had withdrawn from the company, they were not financially liable for anything. They could just move on without being accused of any wrongdoing with their reputation intact.

Nevertheless, we still had to present our case to the judge. John and I were prepared for the hearing and had worked on the documents and the order in which we would present them. John had found old precedents and had been collating all the information for the last two years. He'd even written a script to go along with each point so even if nerves got the better of him, he was still able to continue.

I was feeling happier than I had felt for months. Finally, we would get some closure. Even if we weren't granted a strike out it would hopefully make Commercide accountable for what they had done.

Ideally, I hoped the judge would see we needed to be compensated for all the pain and suffering they had caused us.

Our case was at 10:00am the following day. John looked displeased when he discovered I had booked two rooms for us at the hotel, but I didn't want to risk any fights between us before the morning.

I had expected some Buildadeck staff to be there at the courtroom, especially Paul as I'd hoped he would have been interested to hear what we had to say. John explained to me that it wasn't the hearing and witnesses wouldn't be able to speak. My intention was to beg the judge to let me have my day in court. I was desperate for her to hear what they had done to me. This is the draft I'd written in my head:

"I am not standing here as a lawyer. I am standing here as a person: a woman who's had her life slowly destroyed in the cruellest way. Everyone at Buildadeck and Commercide Ventures knows John and I are not thieves. We didn't break any fiduciary duties and we have never committed fraud.

One of the most disturbing aspects of it all has been all Nick's efforts to terrorise me into giving up my fight through coercion and bullying. It is not an exaggeration to say I have been subjected to a sustained two year-long campaign of pressure, manipulation and intimidation. If this was in a domestic setting it would be a criminal offence. But in a commercial setting these tactics are widespread. They are just the common features of the ruthless businessman and are admired in many ways. It's profit first and human lives last.

Nick's accusations are horrific and unfounded and have resulted in me making several attempts to end my life. He was well aware of my previous mental health struggles and exploited this, sending me threatening emails, warning me the rest of my life would be tied up

in litigation and bullying me into signing documents that relieve his company of any liability for the crimes it has committed.

In addition to this, there has been an under the radar campaign to break me down even further. The subtleties of it are meant to sound trivial and coincidental with the aim of making me look crazy when I attempt to describe them.

Over a period of 14 months, I have had strangers, neighbours and people I thought were friends come to my house and invade my life with one aim in mind: to mentally destabilise me. I've been subjected to a series of what can only be described as mind fucks. This has included six individuals all named Paul who have dropped hints about my case, leaving me feeling watched, exposed and under constant threat.

A negotiator was sent who claimed he was a Freemason to intimidate me by telling me his fellow masons were in the police, our government, the justice system, the health service – basically everywhere. His intention was to scare me to the point where I attempted to take my life. I was suicidal again and was admitted to hospital before I could do myself harm.

When I collected together all the evidence and presented it to the police I was humoured into believing I was being taken seriously. They never looked at the evidence. I was dismissed as being paranoid and some kind of crazy conspiracy theorist.

I have listened to a doctor insisting I was psychotic after one meeting. I have since been diagnosed with PTSD by a team of specialists who I have consulted with for months. My house has been down valued. I was terrorised by a stalker on Christmas Day. John's bank account was frozen.

I do not believe that everything that has happened to me has been coincidental or just innocent misunderstandings. I have been the target of an organised smear campaign in an attempt to break me down, make me feel my fight is unwinnable and to pressure me into giving up. Mental abuse is one of the most painful kinds of abuse there is because it is almost impossible to prove.

Commercide Ventures are not alone in their method of intimidation. An article by a group of academics in America published on the Stanford Law site and an eminent member of the House of Lords have highlighted the unethical tactics private equity firms employ. As Lord Prem Sikka says, this profession needs to be regulated. If it is not and business owners are not given basic protections their criminal practices will continue to go unpunished.

If there's any justice in this world the court will see this for what it is: an abuse of process and a calculated effort to ruin my reputation, deprive me of everything I have worked for over the years and drive me to take my own life. In a way they have succeeded. I have lost my daughter, my husband, my friends and my health because of what this predatory company has done to me. They have turned my life into a living hell."

I never did get to speak these words. In fact, the day was awful.

Judge Kelly entered the courtroom and we all rose. She came in with a man beside her who was a barrister in training. She was pleasant and seemed kind, but she had no tolerance for someone who wanted to speak her mind. It was purely litigation and the presentation of the facts. Not victim statements.

John was happy to represent us. I had taken it for granted that he would present our defence with confidence. He had been rehearsing our day in court for months. In total we had five files and everything was perfectly organised to make it easy for him to refer to the right documents. Unfortunately, he had over-prepared and was so fixated on the fine details he couldn't clearly summarise the important facts.

He had expected to have his say first, but the judge asked him a question which he said "threw him off." He totally lost track over what he had planned to say. He was panicked, red faced, shaking and fumbling for words. I actually thought he was about to have a stroke. He was incoherent and the pressure was too much.

It was awful to watch a normally confident, knowledgeable, articulate person completely lose his confidence in an instant. John is no doubt still suffering PTSD from the Safestyle litigation.

I said some encouraging words to calm his nerves and told him to start where he was comfortable but it was no good. He could barely string a sentence together. I knew we only had one shot at this so I stepped in and began reading from his notes and directing the judge to the relevant pages. I didn't have a clue what any of it meant and couldn't focus. It was like reading from a script that meant nothing to me.

Instead of helping I just made things worse. I could sense the judge's frustration. She said we could have obtained information from the other side if we had requested it. Because we didn't know

the rules, we had only produced half the documents we needed for evidence. I asked the judge if we could take a break and she was happy to accommodate.

We went outside for a cigarette. I was so angry and disappointed with John and told him what I thought but without the anger and intensity I would have displayed in the past. There was no point trying to control the situation. It wasn't a court hearing thank goodness.

I did speak again, but I was full of emotion which was obvious by the sound of my voice. Due to the pressure of the day, I burst into tears and was shocked to hear a noise like a whale come out of my mouth. That's all I could hear. It was two years of pain. It was a pain so intense and unbearable I can't describe it to anyone. But I will never forget how it felt.

The barrister from the other side then had her say. She said the land we had bought to adjoin to our previous house belonged to Buildadeck. I had to hold my tongue. I had paid for that land and given the money to John, but he hadn't put it all into Buildadeck's bank account. All I could think was that I would never look at him the same way ever again. My respect for him all but disappeared that day.

The judge decided there was a lot of evidence and that realistically she needed at least two weeks for us to respond so she could consider her verdict.

The journey home from Leeds was awful. I cried nearly the whole way. I had expected the judge to make her decision there and then and couldn't deal with yet more days spent anxiously waiting for this nightmare to be over.

CHAPTER 32

The Truth About My Relationship with John

I've always lied about the first time John and I had sex because at the time he was married. I've always claimed we got together after he was divorced. But as this book is my "reset" I'm going to be honest now. Nobody has ever heard this part of our story.

John was the original investor in my Magnamole cable threading tool which I talk about in my other book "Mother of Invention." In the beginning he intimidated me. In fact, I described him in my first book as a man who'd had Botox. Not because he'd had the muscle freezing injections – although he could certainly do with them after the past two years – but because his face gives nothing away. You'd never know whether he was sad, happy or distraught. His expression doesn't change.

In the early days I would avoid meeting his gaze., I found it difficult to look into his eyes. He was a professional man and I was scared he'd see straight through me. I had almost no self-esteem and didn't want him to think he'd made a bad choice investing in me and my company.

The first time we met I noticed there was something very intense about him. When he was at his office I would always check first to see if he was standing outside smoking a cigarette. He smoked ten times more than me to cope with his stress. I didn't like smoking with him because then I was forced to speak and I didn't want him to see that he made me nervous. I thought he was so wise in business and also stoic and scary with a stature that commanded respect.

My business operations were based in a large, glass faced building in Leeds, another one of his many investments. He had a chauffeur to drive him to each of his businesses and it was rare that I actually got to see him.

Then late one night I received an email from John responding to a question I had asked him. I was impressed. Like me he was obsessed with work. I know I used to work until 3 or 4:00am. We exchanged a few messages and he asked me to meet him. Wtf did I do now? I was worried because he was my investor. Was it an innocent request? Would I live to regret it if I said no?

We met at the M18 services half way between Scunthorpe and Leeds which was his suggestion not mine. I don't need to say what happened next. It's hard to admit because he was still married.

I drove home riddled with guilt telling myself it was him who had cheated and not me. I didn't have a partner, but it was still wrong. The next day I was full of anxiety. Would the shame be written all over my face? But no, both of us focused on our work and it was business as usual. After this we met a couple more times before John went into hospital for his operation, the aftermath of which nearly killed him.

Then he and his wife moved to Spain as part of his recouperation but split up in March 2013 when they were there. He left with his clothes and his car, got an apartment and stayed in the country for the rest of the year. She retained everything else which included around £200,000 in the bank and house and a flat in the UK worth £250,000, while he had almost nothing.

(Incidentally, when his litigation with Safestyle began she hired a UK-based law firm thinking she would get half the £30 million or so she thought John would receive. After he lost the lawsuit, she claimed they had separated in 2017 even though they were living in separate countries. This was because she'd heard he'd bought Buildadeck and wanted half of that too. She even said I had never worked at the company! I think this is all I need to say about her.)

When he returned from Spain John was like a different man. Having almost died twice as well as spending six months in hospital, his values seemed to have changed. Now he was a single man, so we'd meet up for a bite to eat and a catch up every week or so just as friends. His determination to succeed fascinated me. He'd lost everything yet was driven to start all over again.

I knew that whatever he did he'd be successful because his mind was wired differently. When I really got to know him I saw he had a dry sense of humour that many don't have. He would have me crying with laughter! He saw the world and people differently to anybody else. He was a funny, gentle giant.

In 2017 we rekindled our relationship. The story I've always told others is that he attempted to kiss me three times before I finally gave in. That was true for our second time round. We were sitting in his car when he leaned over to give me a kiss, but I didn't feel that way about him. We laughed about the attempt and I made it clear I wasn't going down that road again. Because he's a chancer he kept trying and I kept rejecting him.

Since breaking with a man I'd nearly married, I'd only ever had short term flings once in a blue moon and always made it clear that my daughter came first, followed by my work. Another problem was what I called the 7-week itch. This was around the time I'd be questioned about how many hours I worked which became annoying. So I just accepted that I would never find anyone who loved their job as much as I did, until John that is.

One night we were at his house in Leeds and I was laid on the floor with my feet up near the fire. We'd been talking about James Caan and also his ordeals with Mitu. I asked him how he was so calm and had no resentment. To my surprise he replied that he had low self-esteem. I was shocked that he'd figured this out. Self-awareness in men is quite a rare thing!

He advised me to let go of the past completely and move on. He said my past was holding me back. This was easier said than done when I hated injustice. I remember saying to him, "You should be my permanent counsellor that I can keep in my pocket!

At this point he made his third attempt to kiss me. But this time it was different. I loved his company, his sense of humour and wisdom. That night he really made me feel that he cared. I let that kiss happen and I spent the night with him. We were both single so I didn't feel bad the next morning. I left that morning with a smile on my face. But I had no expectations of where things would go.

A few days later he invited me out to dinner. I remember it was a Greek restaurant in Leeds. But what I really remember was the words he said. He looked me in the eye and said, "You're actually very clever and speak a lot of sense."

For the first time in my life, I felt heard and understood, but I did tell him that I was worried I'd be too strong a character for him. But we had a relationship similar to my mum and dad with my mum being the stronger of the two. Maybe I'd just chosen the wrong kind of man in the past.

As we were approaching the dreaded 7-week mark I decided to take a holiday on my own to see if I missed him. I didn't know if being away would spoil what we had. When I returned, a phone call with a withheld number came through in his car. He tried to answer it normally, but it was a woman and he quickly had to cut her off because I was there.

My gut told me something was wrong. It took a while for him to be honest. He assured me they'd only had lunch together, but does a leopard ever change its spots? Only John knows the answer to that. I decided because it was so early in the relationship that I would take his word for it and put it to the back of my mind.

There are white lies and deliberate lies. I can always tell when someone isn't telling the truth. John calls me a witch for having this skill. I have blamed myself for being intimidating and have excused John for lying because he feared my reaction. But now I see this as very unfair to me, because not once have I cheated. Even if it hurts, I will always be honest.

CAPITAL PUNISHMENT

CHAPTER 33

Why I Had to End It

Despite any lingering doubts we were married on December 22nd 2018. After this I grew to love John like I had never loved anyone before. People would say how do you manage to live together and work together? But we were happy and it worked.

By now I'd set myself up in business with Paul and was working under the larger Buildadeck umbrella. We grew the business quickly, working to our proven model. I was lucky to have a husband who understood work was my priority and would joke that I had my real husband John and my work husband Paul.

Unfortunately, being a director went to Paul's head and he became arrogant and thought he was better than his staff and his fitters would call me to complain about him. I always had Paul's back and half the time I sorted out the issue without him even being aware.

With the value of hindsight, I know now that I'd changed too. I had taken over as CEO following John's bankruptcy, while also maintaining my sales director role. I was getting bombarded from everywhere. I had the office staff, the fitters, the salespeople, the customers and the suppliers all on my case. The phone never stopped ringing; not only at work, but late into the night. I would probably say I became a right bitch!

The differences between Paul and I became clear when one of our staff became demanding. We were already paying her more than the others because she grafted seven days a week. I got her the car she wanted and she was on an excellent salary, but it wasn't enough.

I was getting calls from park managers and her attendance was no longer consistent, plus her attitude had changed. One day I called her out on her behaviour and she went running to Paul to complain about me. I was mortified when she handed in her notice and I blamed myself for it.

A few weeks later the truth came out. All the time she led us to believe she was doing her work she was setting up her own company! If I'd known she had wanted to start her own business I would have helped her. In fact, an employee of ours called Shane did the same thing but he went about it all in the right way. The handover was done properly, we supplied him with raw materials and I gave him some parks to help him on his way.

Paul blamed me for this woman's exit because of the friction between us. Like I said, he had changed and I didn't like who he'd become. But his behaviour didn't bother John. I wondered if it was because he didn't want to ruin our working relationship, but it was becoming a problem. Paul had been petulant on more than one occasion and could be immature if you disagreed with him.

He had extended our fit time from 7 days to more like 14. I could live with one or two days because nobody had complained, but he'd introduced these terms without John or I knowing. When I started getting complaints I was shocked by how much he'd let things slide. John sided with Paul because he didn't want to lose him. He didn't hear my voice or defend me.

CAPITAL PUNISHMENT

After struggling through the Covid era, Paul was now working a fraction of the hours we did. John and I were now working 7 days a week and sometimes 14-hour days. My resentment towards John and Paul was building and after we closed the window company it became difficult to work with either of them.

John had bought LUPA Windows at the same time as Buildadeck. Because our workers weren't allowed to go inside people's homes it was impossible to keep it running. Unfortunately, we didn't qualify for any of the government's £69 billion to help businesses survive during the lockdowns because Commercide Ventures was an American firm. We should have probably convinced Nick to keep it, but nobody knew when things would return to normal.

In June 2020, Nick told us he had no choice but to offload it. Making the decision to shut down the company and informing our staff of 150 took its toll on me. Some had come from families that had worked there for generations, like the father and son who'd made uPVC windows all their lives. Thankfully most of the workers found new jobs.

At the time we were hated for delivering the news. It didn't matter who'd made the decision, John and I were seen as the ones in charge and took the brunt of the blame. Some of the employees were lovely and knew it wasn't our fault, but others weren't so understanding. We received death threats. Our home address was published online and I lived in fear that one day someone would creep up from behind and attack me.

Being an empath, I worried myself sick about what people thought of me. It didn't matter what anyone said to reassure me, I hated this part of my character. I was getting around two hours' sleep a night and barely eating. I was thinking dark thoughts and the only way I coped was knowing if it got any worse, I could always take my life. I could pull myself back most of the time, but I was only just scraping by.

The shock of having to let go of so many people, the pandemic, the lockdowns and working all the hours god sent took a toll on my health. Tensions were also high between Paul, John and myself and former employees were saying terrible things about us on social media.

As a result of all this I spent two weeks in August 2020 as an inpatient at The Priory during Covid, recovering from a nervous breakdown. Thankfully I still had private health insurance because that place is not cheap.

John had taken Paul's side, and in my opinion, it fractured our relationship. We did repair it after I'd spent time in rehab, but things were never the same. I recall that when John left me at the hospital all he said was, "Take care. Look after yourself," like I was some distant relative.

After I came home and was feeling ready to start working again, Paul and John told me they didn't want me back in the business, which I found quite insulting. John said he thought it was in my best interest that I didn't return and there'd be less conflict. Plus, it was easier than facing the issues with Paul that needed to be addressed. So I was forced to resign from Buildadeck, although I kept my position as director.

My absence affected the integrity of the business. After I left because the lead times were further extended, the team work we'd built became fractured and greed crept its way back with price hikes.

The way I saw it was John felt he had had the best out of me and had reached the end of my usefulness. I resented John for his lack of support and still can't forgive him for it to this day. He took away my purpose, my passion and the reason I got out of bed every day. What was I supposed to do now? We had always been a team and now he'd ditched me.

A few days before our disastrous court appearance asking the judge for a strike out, I told John that our marriage was in tatters and I wanted a divorce. We both knew it was coming as we hadn't shared a bed for a year. My nerves were so shredded that every little sound seemed to be amplified: his breathing, his eating and even the sound of his voice. I didn't realise at the time this is one of the effects of trauma. When you're constantly in fight or flight mode all your senses become heightened.

Upon hearing the news, John went silent and his face showed no expression as usual. I couldn't tell if he was even slightly upset, although I imagine he must have felt something. He didn't even react or try to stop me when I took off my wedding rings, packed up a few clothes and went to live with my dad in my childhood home a few miles away.

When we arrived at our hotel in Leeds the night before the hearing for the strike out it was confirmed that our marriage really was over as I had told John to book separate rooms. I couldn't risk us getting angry with each other on the morning he presented our case to the judge in case it knocked his confidence. It made no difference anyway because his nerves got the better of him on the day.

Unfortunately, this legal battle involves two completely different kinds of egos and characters. Nick is brash and loud and has evil running through his veins

and would probably sell his grandma if it meant he could make money. Then there's John who is honest, retiring and tends to overthink everything. Rather than speak out clearly in simple terms, he convinced himself the legal documents he'd brought would defend us.

But people don't relate so much to written words, especially if they involve accounts or lots of legal phrases. They react more to what they hear and how it's delivered. That's why politicians don't have to be honest. All they have to do is deliver their lies with absolute confidence. As the saying goes, people would rather believe a simple lie than the complicated truth.

At the time I pitied John after we left that courtroom. He'd lost me. He had possibly lost our home and he'd lost some of my respect. He would constantly bitch and moan about people and happily load the gun, then sit back and say and do nothing. I lost count how many times I told him he didn't have a backbone. He was like this with the architects too. I was sick of wearing the trousers in the relationship.

Plus, I still could not believe he had played right into Commercide's hands by failing to pay the entire £30,000 I had sent him to put into Buildadeck's bank account. That £5,000 shortfall was pure hold to Nick's forensic accounts who used it as proof that we were stealing from the company.

Why hadn't he learned his lessons from Safestyle and Mitu? He was another one who avoided putting anything in writing. John could have drafted the agreement about my deferred consideration being paid off incrementally through the purchase of materials over the 14 months via the company and asked Nick to sign them. If Nick had refused this would have clearly signalled that he might use the arrangement against us.

John rationalises this by saying he did not need Nick's permission because as far as he was concerned, Commercide was only holding his shares until he asked for them back, which meant he was the chief decision maker.

During his leadership he estimates that we had grown the business from £6m to £24m, so paying off what Buildadeck owed me was not a problem. He never imagined Nick would lie and say he didn't know that I was being paid. Therefore, he never considered a written agreement to be necessary.

John and I have both learned so much from the past few years going through hell. Sadly, the love we both had for each other eroded to the point I knew we had to part ways. Who knows, maybe if we hadn't experienced the last two years maybe we'd still be together. Despite everything, we still talk on the phone and see each other often. Our legal battles will keep us together for the foreseeable future.

I will miss being his wife, but to me John is no longer the man I thought he was. Most importantly, I cannot forget all the times I didn't feel his love. If I ever share my life with a man again, I'll need more and I won't apologise for that.

CAPITAL PUNISHMENT

CHAPTER 34

My Friends' Gaslighting Is Revealed
(No - I am Not Crazy!)

After the court fiasco I drove straight to the hospital to see my dad. Once again, the doctors suspected he had sepsis, an infection on his heart or food poisoning, the same as before.

I had no faith that they really knew what he had after what had happened with John earlier that year, so I decided to move back home to live with my dad. I needed to keep an eye on him and time to reflect on my relationship with John.

I made the decision to move out the night after the court case. I didn't want to vent my rage and disappointment on John like I had done in the past. I was growing as a person and knew I'd made the right choice. As soon as my head touched the pillow I slept soundly. That hadn't happened for the last two years since we were fired from Buildadeck.

I responded to a comment on TikTok that my dad was in hospital and received texts from both Rita and Gerry. I hadn't heard from Gerry in months. Rita and Susan had both been asking me for news on the court case but I'd ignored them. I wanted to tell them both to leave me alone but I was interested to see if they would reveal their gameplan. My patience was about to pay off.

Rita was insistent and asked, "You not talking to me?"

"I am insulted you think I am so stupid. You, Gerry, Marcus and Paul (SAS man) will all get karma," I replied.

"What??? What have I said? And when have I said you're stupid? Wtf!"

"You all think I'm thick. That's the funny bit because I'm one step ahead. Paul and Marcus telling stories about the Freemasons… You with the sunflowers. You're all sad little fucks."

Rita responded, "Are you talking about me?? Coz I fucking hope not!"

Just after midnight after she'd had time to think about things, Rita realised I'd sussed her out so she sent me another text message.

"Me giving you sunflowers? Are you joking? I never bought you any sunflowers."

I called John just to make sure I wasn't imagining things. He'd seen them with his own eyes. He was as shocked as I was that Rita denied buying the flowers. At that moment the penny dropped for him too. He realised that she was part of an elaborate scheme to make me look insane.

At 8:25am she sent me this concerned-sounding voicemail message:

"Sharon will you please talk to me. I'm really, really worried. I don't know what's happened in court. You know that I didn't send the flowers. The sunflowers were already in the vase [when I came over in the morning]. I don't understand what's gone wrong from us having a lovely meal together to you accusing us of being one of them. You know I am not one of them Sharon. I have supported you through thick and thin and that's not changed.

I'm worried about you and John and the whole situation. I'm worried that you've been pushed too far with the court case… I don't care what you said because of where your head's at. You know it's not true. I haven't done anything. I never have and I never will… I hope you feel better… We are not involved, you know that and I damn well know it 100%. Okay love you. Bye."

Let me tell you about Rita. She was my childminder for my daughter Molly from the age of three to around ten. Many years later when she broke up with her partner we resumed our friendship. At that time I had an eating disorder and was struggling.

Rita didn't have many friends who were able to go out with her in the evenings. This was something I'd done in my younger days, but not anymore. I'd rather be single than go out drinking to oblivion. I'd already cancelled once and when we planned to go out again I just didn't want to go. I was struggling mentally and had lost so much weight I wanted to stay hidden. So I sent her a text apologising that I couldn't make it. She responded, "Two strikes and you're out. Don't ever contact me again!" and blocked me.

I didn't have the courage to go over and speak to her and accepted that our friendship was over. When she eventually got back in touch I knew I could never cancel or let her down because of the brutal consequences.

CAPITAL PUNISHMENT

After I told her I'd figured out what she, Marcus, Gerry and SAS Paul had been up to she would have been fuming. The fact she left me the long placatory voicemail was confirmation that I was completely right about them all. Given her past reactions she would have sent a short, angry line and cut me off.

Then Gerry's text arrived. "Keep going strong Sharon. Don't let the bastards grind you down. Here for a chat if you need me."

My response was short and sweet. "Fuck off, don't push me."

He responded with "What? Answer your phone, I want to talk to you."

"Fuck off! I'm waiting for my book's final edits. You're all in it." I said.

"What you on about," he replied, playing dumb.

"I'm just writing my story with all the facts and the timeline so people can decide for themselves what you've all been doing."

"I don't know what the hell you're on about."

"That's even worse. Not admitting what you've all done. You thought I wouldn't figure things out for myself. You took my kindness for weakness. I am blocking you."

Everyone that turned against me had received something from me. I had never asked for anything in return other than appreciation. Instead, they all got together to make sure I learned the lesson that "no good deed goes unpunished." They wanted to see if they could mentally break me down until I was beyond repair. At a guess I'd say it was SAS Paul that had briefed them well on the art of gaslighting.

Gerry will remember when at Christmas he had no money and how I had gone to the supermarket with Rita and filled the trolley full of Christmas turkey, drinks, sweets and everything to make sure he had a lovely time like everyone deserves. He will also recall the time when he couldn't afford to pay an accountant to do his taxes, so I paid for them to be done. In his times of need I'd always helped him out.

Before I blocked him, he said, "You seriously need help. I'm coming over to see you at your dad's to sort this out this evening."

I responded, "I will call the police if you come anywhere near."

"I guess your court case didn't end well," he said sarcastically.

He was using the same line as Rita! Taunting me about the court case and hoping to see signs of a breakdown. They were going down the road of I've lost the plot and finally cracked. In reality the exact opposite happened. I saw everything for what it was with total clarity.

As soon as I blocked Gerry he must have jumped straight on the phone to Rita to inform her about our conversation because she decided to have one last pop at me before she too was blocked.

"Heard you've been bad mouthing me and saying I'm a bitch and involved in trying to take you down. Are you fucking having a laugh? I never bought the fucking sunflowers and you fucking know it… Do not tell lies about me or I will go fucking mental after being the only one that's had your back through this... I think you need to retract the sunflower comments as you well know I never bought the fucking things. To say I'm fucking fuming is an understatement."

I replied, "Ask Gerry for proof of the texts where I call you a bitch. I'm sick and tired of people talking shit. Leave me alone or I will go to the police. Everyone needs to back off and leave my name out your mouths."

"You still need to admit I never bought those flowers. Go to the police. They are useless anyway," she responded angrily.

"You bought the flowers! Why are you lying? They were sunflowers and you bought them."

This was my last message to her. All of them were playing the innocent until the very end. Liars, confidence tricksters and con artists, each every one of them. I hope they enjoyed playing their little game. They all deserved each other.

CHAPTER 35

Nick's False Statements to The British Business Bank

One of the clauses of the Settlement Agreement we signed with Buildadeck was that we could not make a "subject access request." This is when an individual asks for a copy of any personal data that organisation is using or storing that concerns them. In the UK the legislation states that anyone has the right to request details or copies of this information and it must be provided within 30 days.

John had recalled that Nick had often referred to the British Business Bank, so we wrote to them on 16th June 2024. They replied on 18th July 2024 that they were not prepared to disclose the information saying, "Your personal data we hold pertains to our management forecasting and planning. We have concluded that the release of this information would prejudice the conduct of our business."

Not satisfied with this response we challenged it and threatened to refer the matter to The Information Commissioner's Office. We didn't expect to hear anything back from them and put the matter out of our minds. Then out of the blue on 27th February 2025, three days before our strike out application, we received a detailed response to John's request.

Here are the key extracts from the British Business Bank's response to the request of John Ross:

4th December 2020

"The fund currently controls all the equity but has an agreement to allocate 70% to John Ross.

18th April 2023

"The main concern noted by interested parties was the background to the bankruptcy of John Ross, the CEO."

We know this statement is untrue because one bidder who was interested in buying Buildadeck told us they had the backing of six banks, none of whom had a problem with John's bankruptcy. It was clear to anyone that John's bankruptcy was the result of the Safestyle litigation and not the result of financial mismanagement or wrongdoing.

23 June 2023

"The CEO John Ross, who was responsible for preparing the business for sale had mismanaged the process. We decided to remove him as director and shareholder."

This is clearly false also. The real reason he was terminated was that their accountancy firm had mismanaged the sale of Buildadeck by overpromising on sale value. They had set Commercide's price expectation at £30 million. (Deliberately overvaluing a company and/or misrepresenting its debt are other areas that require regulation.)

John had told them £15 million to £20 million would be a good result and for this he was accused of plotting to try to steal the company "on the cheap." With independent valuations coming in at between £16 and £17 million, John was proved to be right.

18 December 2023

"[We] are taking legal action against the previous CEO, John Ross [and another], for misappropriation of around £400k of cash for personal matters... as he has already been through a bankruptcy process."

This final comment was dated 18th December 2023, which is three days after their application for a freezing order against us. In my opinion it looks like an afterthought to justify their actions to the bank.

The reply to my request to the British Business Bank was left blank, which suggests Nick never mentioned anything about me or Paul. There were no comments about the acquisition of our company, no mention of payments to me and no accusations of theft or fraud.

That is because he knows I am guilty of neither.

CAPITAL PUNISHMENT

CHAPTER 36

Nick's Fictional Case Against Us

In April 2023, just before John was ousted from Buildadeck there was a phone call between him, Nick and another member of Commercide. He was asked not to record the conversation, but he did so for his own protection as Nick was generally opposed to putting anything in writing unless it suited him.

Also, we were aware of his aggressive, browbeating and insulting manner. Nick had previously referred to other business owners as "thieving robbing bastards." For example, in 2020 we were on a conference call with the managing director of the company that provided us with an invoice discounting facility. Because Nick didn't agree with their fees, he hurled a torrent of abuse at this poor woman and told her she could he "Stick her facility [where the sun don't shine]."

Here is a transcript of the call:

NICK: So John, every conversation we've had since we got over there last week and other investigations bring up one impropriety after another. Blatant lies, misappropriation, breach of fiduciary responsibility, I would certainly argue fraud, and conflict of interest.

We can only assume he is referring to the payments of deferred consideration and the purchase of the building materials,

because no evidence of any of these other allegations has ever been produced.

NICK: It's actually mind boggling to me, having been doing this for 40 years, the behaviour. It's one example of bad behaviour after another. I've never seen anything like it. So at the end of the day your choices are this. We will let you keep the money we believe was stolen, because it's Sharon's money. Whatever, we believe that money was stolen. You can keep the money and walk away quietly and we'll come up with a script to tell management.

We have wondered how many times he's delivered this spiel. It was as if it was rehearsed and came straight from the "Nick Smith Book of Phony Complaints and False Accusations." On the one hand he says, "It' Sharon's money," and on the other he is accusing us of stealing it. He knew this money was well overdue for payment.

NICK: Anything else besides… is going away. There's no equity value added because you can't even sell the company. So equity, everything, directorships, that's all gone… If you refuse that, it doesn't work for you, we're gonna we're coming after you and Sharon legally… because she's not responsible for returning that money… We will seek a claw back of that money and other damages against both of you.

So we can either do this in a somewhat dignified manner, given what's gone on, or it can become a big shit show… which we wanna avoid, which is why we're not gonna claw back the money and start that legal action if you agree, both of you, because obviously Sharon's a director or there's some entanglement and thinking what's best interest of the company because given your behaviour, obviously from a standpoint of the market, the company is not financeable or saleable.

It was obvious that Buildadeck had been massively overvalued. Two bidders had approached John individually and said Nick's accountants had told them "You will need a new management team because of John's bankruptcy." They had both said this was a strange point to make and they disagreed with it. In fact, they said they would only proceed if John remained. They also confirmed that the banks were keen for John to remain as CEO.

As evidence of this, one of the bidders stated in their written offer dated 10th February 2023, "We are very excited about the opportunity and would be keen to partner with John Ross, Paul Jones and the broader management team as a fundamental stakeholder to further develop the business".

NICK: "Management's not stupid and also, if you don't agree, we are going to sit down with them and walk them through all the issues we found that we have accurate documentation for, so they know exactly what's going on. So there's no bullshit about people spreading rumours of who's doing what. It's very concrete what you did.

This is a ridiculous threat because the management team was already aware of everything. As part of this team, we didn't hide anything from them. Two years after Nick's accusations, Commercide still hasn't produced a single piece of evidence to prove we have done anything wrong. Nick claims, "We are going to walk [the management team] through the issues we found. This documentation came from management! They

already knew what was going on as we had discussed Sharon's deferred consideration situation with them repeatedly.

JOHN: Do you mind sharing these allegations with me?

NICK: Well, you know, I will share some but the fact that you've been asked and you keep denying it is offensive, but sure, I'll kick in a few, but…

JOHN: Just put it in writing if you want.

NICK: I don't need to put anything in writing, John. You know what you did and if you wanna fuck with us and particularly me, given the opportunities I've given you, you're gonna spend your last days with lawsuits and Sharon as well. I don't know where you think you're going with this but I'm not putting anything in writing. You know what you did.

UK employment law stipulates that as part of any disciplinary process the "employer" must provide the "employee" with a written record of the allegations made against them. There should also be a formal investigation to which the accused has a right of reply. There should also be an appeals process. Nick did not comply with any of this because as he'd once said, "I don't give a fuck about English Law."

NICK: … You sent the report in to the HMRC, who by the way, are not moving forward unless you're gone, because of your behaviour. There is a proposal in front of the HMRC that was provided in the summer where it was clear that there would be no deferred compensation payments made. Not only did you then make them after that, but you increased them… Even little things, like he didn't even know you were married to Sharon… I mean, the whole thing's a fucking shit show, John. What bits do you want me to go through? That you don't think you misbehaved and breached your fiduciary responsibility?

Nick is referring to a report produced by Commercide's tax advisors. It is true the company owed taxes to HMRC., During Covid the company did not qualify for any of the loans offered by the UK government as it was (at least on paper) majority owned by an American company.

As we were non-operational through no fault of our own, I asked Nick for financial support. He said, "Sorry we can't. You'll have to defer the tax." Like many companies trying to survive during the pandemic we arranged a deal with HMRC to defer payments going forward. This arrangement was due to be re-negotiated and Nick's advisors had drafted a report in support of this.

There is also a section in this report that states the Directors (me and Paul) would have our deferred consideration payments delayed until HMRC had been repaid. John told Nick's tax advisors this had never been agreed to and honestly, why would it have been? This report was not produced by the company, approved by the company, and as far as we know was never put in front of HMRC.

It was John's responsibility to manage the company's finances and to ensure creditors got paid. I think he did this quite well given the constraints he had to work within. Companies House Records show cash at bank grew by £1.6m between 2021 and 2022. To put it into context, as a company grows everything

grows. Between 2021 and 2022 turnover was up by 60%, our creditors grew by 31% and our tax liabilities grew by 26%

The fact that John was married to me was completely irrelevant, so it never crossed his mind to specifically mention this detail to Nick's tax advisor. In keeping with his gameplan, Nick is making a serious issue out of a total non-issue. His line of attack was, "You've done some bad things, but I am not going to tell you what they are."

The whole thing *is* a shit show. Anyone can take anyone to court in this country, make wild allegations, throw some money at fancy lawyers and there you have it: a two-year legal battle and all the stress and trauma that goes with it. The one thing Nick didn't bank on was my tenacity. Even with all the lies, coercion, bullying and threats and people telling me to walk away, I will not back down. My integrity is the most important thing to me and I will fight to defend it until my dying breath.

NICK: …You wanna play this game and fuck around, we're gonna sell shares immediately and you're out. So I'm offering you a chance to keep the money and have some dignity. But if I stand in the way and I sit down with management and walk them through it and we start litigation we're gonna take the shares and accelerate anyway.

I'm really trying to keep this low key. Frankly, me, if it was me personally, I wouldn't even offer this, I'd claw back the money, but I'm thinking about the company and it's embarrassing enough for me, given the list of indiscretions… You don't realise the ramifications of this for you guys personally when you say things.

Then also there's this draft report of a new proposal where you claim hardship, you haven't paid us the first half, which is an unsecured claim because of hardship and then you state to HMRC that Commercide is not deferring interest and those are two of the three reasons why you need all these deferrals. I mean, are you fucking kidding me? Are you just gonna deny that?

JOHN: I'm not gonna deny anything. But what I am gonna say is that that proposal should not have gone anywhere and when HMRC came up with the point about us saying we wouldn't take deferred consideration, I said to him that

I had no idea where that came from. That should never have been in there, and that he'd better come up with a solution for removing it. It's not my drafted report...

As was stated before, this was not our accountant's drafted report. When we heard Nick's tax advisors had suggested Paul and I should not take any deferred consideration we objected because ours was the oldest debt in the company. We told Nick's advisor to delete that stipulation and re-write it to reflect the truth. The next version came back saying we would suffer "hardship" if we were not paid, so he was told to rewrite the report. In the end Buildadeck still owes me £300,000.

NICK: Regardless, John, come on, we could go back. There's so many different things John. I mean, come on. You hid things from us; you hid things from HMRC; you hid things from management... you don't communicate. You do what you wanna do. There is zero basis for sending that money out. We offered for you to return the money and maybe things would be different, but you refused.

I know you think Sharon doesn't have to return it because she did nothing wrong. You're making a big mistake on that one, but that's your opinion and you've got your ego and you think you're right. I know you now so... I'm not trying to convince you otherwise. I'm just gonna try to convince you you're bankrupt... Those legal bills are gonna get paid by somebody...

He was trying to bully us. He knows he gave permission for those deferred consideration payments to be made. What he is trying to do is play on John's one weakness, his desire to protect me. He knows John didn't have anything (yet Nick still went for a freezing order on him) so he suggests lots of legal fees that I will have to pay.

There is an often-used expression in legal circles, "Play the man not the ball" in other words when the facts (the ball) are not there, focus on the man and he will cave eventually. Again, this tactic will not work with me. It may have worked initially when I was in shock, but not now.

JOHN: There's a difference between won't repay it and can't repay it.

I don't know why John said that because repaying it was never a consideration. The money I'd been paid was rightfully mine. It had been outstanding since at least 2019. What I now find bizarre is that having paid Nick over £7 million in interest on his £15 million loan, Nick felt we'd had more than we were entitled to and he'd somehow ended up out of pocket!

NICK: That's bullshit. You should have paid this. You should repay it. The money's somewhere. With what we're offering, you don't have to repay it. We just want you to go quietly. If you don't, okay, that's a shame, because everyone in the company's gonna know what you did and we're gonna have lawyers all over the place. This is gonna be a wasted expense for me. I don't wanna waste money. I know I'm gonna win, but it's expensive.

JOHN: Yeah.

NICK: And it's a distraction. You drained money out of the company when you knew taxes were due. That's just shameful behaviour. Taxes had to get paid and we had to get paid and you gave the money to your wife. That alone, John, is
beyond excusable, no matter what you say. And that happened, that's a fact. So that alone is a reason for all of this, besides a long list of other things we have.

As I said previously, the taxes got paid; they got paid and I got paid. The only issue is that I got paid later than everyone else. If anyone had a grievance it should be me. All this happened at the same time as the company's cash reserves grew by £1.6m. What Nick seems to forget is they bought my business which was making over £1m a year in profit. The company was growing and it was debt free. Now he's complaining that they actually paid some of what they owed me!

JOHN: Well, you're not giving me anything to contemplate.

NICK: I am giving you something to contemplate. First of all, if you're thinking of contemplating any economics between what the British Business Bank now knows and what HMRC now knows and everybody else, there's not a hell of a chance, even if we wanted to, and I don't, and there's no money in the company to pay any compensation to you because you took that, and as far as your equity, you just saw in the market, it's worthless.

I always paid the taxes when they were due. As we have now discovered, my name was not even mentioned to the British Business Bank.

NICK: All our equity is worthless. That's a fact and frankly, that's your fault. I've given you every opportunity and it's clear on the market that because of your background the company's not marketable. That is indisputable, backed by another third party. We have all these various entities here who are all looking at you right now and you're not innocent.

This is complete fabrication. Two bidders said they would like John to stay on as CEO and would be happy to work with him. Their banks also agreed they had no issue with his bankruptcy.

No one's giving you cash for sure. The equity is worthless. The only thing that we could do to offer you something is to not claw back that money and we are quite confident we have a legal case to do that. Will it cost us money to get it, no doubt. Will it cost Sharon money to fight it? For sure. We've got more money...

Another blatant threat. Even though we agreed to their demands to walk away with what we had and no more, they took legal action anyway.

NICK: Sharon got paid improperly by the way of salary because she did not do work. That's another issue for the tax authority, because she's gotten a salary for work she did not do. So that's another exposure and another area of claw back which I didn't even bring up. But we're gonna let all that go and you can keep it. The trade is we want you to go with some dignity and quietly so that there's less disruption in the company.

After I resigned in 2020 it was agreed that I would continue as a director. We recorded Nick agreeing to that and the salary. The tax issues are bogus. All the tax was paid. In fact, I probably paid more than I should have. It wasn't the most tax efficient process.

NICK: So we are offering you something, John, and right now. We've got a company that's got all kinds of problems. We can't finance it. We can't sell it. I know that's not as much an issue for you as it is for me, but that's the reality we are dealing with right now. Beyond the embarrassment of having to explain to

the British government all the details. When they told us a long time ago, you know, frankly we shouldn't have allowed you to stay, but that's on me. The cars, all the fucking shit you guys did. You know, you ran this thing like it was your personal company.

Yes, it was run like it was our business because it was. It has been proven Commercide had no idea how to run it so we had to. In relation to the British Business Bank there was nothing in their disclosure to corroborate what Nick says.

When we questioned him about the amount of debt the British Business Bank wrote off when LUPA went into liquidation, Nick became defensive. During a contract negotiation where we demanded the amount of debt be specified, he suggested If we didn't take his word for it he would get someone else to run the company.

We received offers of £16 million and £17 million which should have resulted in significant equity value. Nick fabricated the amount of debt due to Commercide to make it appear our equity was much smaller.

JOHN: No.

NICK: I'm really sorry it's ended up this way because I believe you're a good operator, that's why I've stuck with you, but it's one thing after another, John. I say with all sincerity that this was the last thing I ever thought. Every day it's been clear evidence of bad behaviour, whether you agree, or not, it's well documented.

Not long after John acquired the business in 2016, Nick began to use the phrase, "You're a good operator." Over the years this accolade grew to the extent Nick would refer to John as, "one of the best operators I've ever worked with." He still is to this day!

NICK: You don't listen. We came last week you said you were figuring out what your story is and the next fucking morning you get management together and you're gonna be stepping back, Paul's gonna be stepping up… You can't help yourself; you just do whatever you want. When I heard that I'm like "Are you fucking kidding me?"

JOHN: Hmm. There were a few things, obviously I misunderstood from last week.

NICK: We're gonna need a few days to figure it out and we'll come back to you but you start talking to people. You've put us in a very difficult situation, because really, at the end of the day, we all want what's best for the business. We have 400 employees.

As has been a consistent feature of this diatribe, Nick is exaggerating. The number of employees was 197. More annoyingly he is trying to suggest he is in some way concerned about them. In 2020 he needlessly closed LUPA UK and with the stroke of a pen put 235 people out of work.

NICK: HMRC, given what was reported, that's an enormous problem, John and you and Sharon are right in their radar. We can work to stop that one but I'm just pointing out between the government and the HMRC there's no salvaging this with you. It's too much.

The HMRC company position has been explained earlier. In terms of my personal tax, I have no issues. This is another example of Nick's blatant smear campaign, which has been concocted out of lies, false accusations and the twisting of facts.

NICK: So I would hope, you know, you're not gonna take a suicidal path out of this. It's a lot of money that was given to Sharon in the last year, plus your salaries and everything else, so there's no sympathy there.

This is a horrific statement knowing my fragile mental health. The casual mention of suicide and him implying he'd have no sympathy if I was dead is as low as anyone can get and illustrates how psychopathic Nick is.

JOHN: OK, well, I've heard what you've said.

NICK: We wanna know by tonight what you're doing because we need to get the lawyers going and everything else... This deal is temporary... John, it's gonna be [pressure] from a lot of different parties. You got a lot of tax people snooping around you and Sharon.

JOHN: But you're just...

NICK: I'm not threatening. I'm not threatening anything. I'm just telling you the shit that's gone on. We want this to go away.

JOHN: But you just...

NICK: But on the other hand...

JOHN: You just dropped a huge bombshell on me and you want me to tell you tonight?

NICK: Yeah, I do, because you've dropped a huge bombshell on us for a long time... Nobody wants to wait any more. So yeah, I do, because we're enforcing
and taking everything as we speak. So the only question is do you wanna litigate or do you wanna walk away and keep the money? That's the trade. There's no other options.

JOHN: Hmm. That's not a decision I can make right now.

NICK: Okay, well if we don't hear by tonight, we will take that as a "No." We don't want you in the office tomorrow, actually, any more. We can work out a way if you need to clean things up, and all that, and have a talk, you know to figure out something. But it's very disruptive now, there's a lot of uneasiness. We need to think about the business.

JOHN: Yeah.

NICK: If you don't wanna tell us tonight, I'd like to know now that you're not gonna come in tomorrow, or else we might have to rescind our first offer, quite frankly...

JOHN: Like I say, you've just dropped a bombshell on me, so I will come back to you with something tonight... I presume we'd do it in some sort of compromise agreement anyway...

NICK: Yes. We would document it, yes.

Given this call was Nick's idea, it is obvious he'd prepared what he had to say and had probably written notes. The speed, intensity and aggression with which Nick delivered his message was like a war manoeuvre. John was ambushed by all Nick's shocking accusations and left reeling as he was bombarded with one falsehood and threat after the next.

Every time John tried to speak, Nick interrupted. The one thing I will say in John's defence is he kept his cool to the end. John says having had time to reflect on all the facts he would love to have this conversation with Nick again because this time he'll be prepared.

John and I discussed Nick's call long into the night. John was adamant it was just blood and bluster and Nick had nothing to blame him for. He pointed out that we had a massive claim for unfair dismissal. They still owed me money from my deferred

consideration and the company was built on our blood sweat and tears, not theirs.

"Fuck em," John said. "We should fight all the way." But I was tired. All the shit we'd been through, not just this, but with his health, the architect and the house build, it was time to take stock. We were both mid to late 50s. John's health was not great and neither of us knew how long we had left, so I said we should just walk away.

We had come to hate the house and at nearly 6,000 sq. ft. it was far too big for just the two of us. We could sell it, buy a nice little house somewhere nearer to Molly and the grandkids and either start a small business or work part time.

I called Nick to say we would agree to his terms.

On the 7th April 2023 Commercide held a number of secret meetings and used their power under the banking documents to seize mine and Paul's shares. Then they had a shareholders' meeting where they used these and John's 70% to vote to remove the directors and appoint four members of Commercide to replace them. Four days later John and I were fired by email with the reason cited as "gross misconduct."

CHAPTER 37

Why We Will Probably Never Receive a Penny in Damages

In order to freeze our bank accounts and stop me selling my house, Buildadeck had to agree to the court that they would compensate John and myself if these injunctions were unjustifiably granted.

When their accusations of theft, fraud and failure of fiduciary duties prove to be baseless, the company must guarantee that an unlimited amount in damages is available. To show they were able to meet this requirement at the end of 2023, Buildadeck produced their financial accounts for the year ending September 2022, which was John's last year as CEO.

On December 4th 2024 we asked the court that Buildadeck proved it was still in a position to meet its obligation to pay damages. This is because Buildadeck has not filed any accounts with Companies House since September 2022. Instead, they extended their year-end report deadline by six months which companies are allowed to do once every five years.

The day their accounts were due, they used a loophole in the Companies Act to shorten their year-end by one day. This extended their deadline for filing by another three months. I say this is a loophole because there's no limit to the number of times it can be done. They could do this every three months for the next 30 years!

Another reason we are questioning their financial status is because Buildadeck has put all five of its subsidiary companies into liquidation. The liquidator's report shows debts totalling £18 million. As Buildadeck had guaranteed to cover its liabilities, it is now insolvent to the tune of around £12.5 million because their 2022 balance sheet showed £5.5 million in assets.

According to a British Business Bank document, Commercide confirmed they were holding a 70% shareholding in Buildadeck for John. My guess is that to avoid having to pay him for his shares, they transferred the ownership of Buildadeck to Commercide Ventures the day they terminated our employment.

Under British company law the directors of Buildadeck, which include members of Commercide, namely Nick and his three American buddies are personally liable for any debts Buildadeck incurs from the date it becomes insolvent.

On February 21st 2025 I couldn't sleep. As usual, I was watching TikTok when I received what I call a "spiritual download." This is like a sudden influx of information and I have no idea where it comes from. All I know is the messages are clear. I think my awareness of something "greater" out there has led to my sensitivity to such things.

I immediately woke John up and told him to check his emails. There it was: confirmation from Companies House that Commercide was no longer directly involved in Buildadeck and its ownership had been transferred to a new company called The Buildadeck Group Ltd.

Further emails confirmed that Nick and his henchmen had all resigned. How convenient. This means if the judge orders a payment into court Buildadeck can stop trading and any legal repercussions will be the responsibility of Paul and the other directors.

This means Nick gets away with his terror tactics and lies. This is how predatory private equity firms operate. Any unsuccessful decisions made at the top are driven to the bottom, leaving any debtors, like myself and John, unpaid.

Here is a brief glimpse into the quagmire that is the legal system where debating the rules of the legal process diverts time and money away from addressing the actual facts of the matter:

On March 19th 2025 we sent a letter to the judge telling her that Buildadeck had failed to comply with the judge's order and we stated they could not meet any award the court might make in relation to damages for wrongfully imposing freezing orders on us.

We requested that they were ordered to pay the court £500,000 within 14 days as security. We also stated that we would object to any evidence they wished to bring outside of the time they'd been given. The court had ordered it within 14 days and they had failed.

On March 24th John submitted his 13th witness statement in response to the freezing orders that were granted on the 21st of December 2023. He told the judge that Buildadeck had not filed any accounts for the previous 30 months. Despite a supposed "management buyout," no detailed financial information had been produced. The records do however show that Commercide Ventures was no longer in control.

He also stated that Buildadeck had played the system to avoid filing properly audited accounts and stated that these were not the actions of a claimant with nothing to hide.

In my opinion Nick set out to divide and conquer. He knew my weaknesses as well as John's and exploited them. I was loyal, honest and too nice, never wanting to upset him. I believe he spotted an opportunity and knew from day one how he intended to manipulate us and then exploited John's bankruptcy so he could walk away with millions.

CHAPTER 38

More Threats and Intimidation

On 11th April 2025 I received a "Notice of Breach and Cease and Desist" from Commercide Ventures. They informed me that I was in breach of the Settlement Agreement I had signed on May 5th 2023 and was liable to pay back my severance pay of £37,500 plus legal costs.

It was laughable that its CEO Nick Smith was accusing me of defamation of character having invented a whole slew of reasons why I am a thief. Now he was using those lies to steal millions from both John and myself.

He was unhappy because I had been posting videos online describing the devious way he has not only stolen our business and shares, but is now staking a claim on my house. Of course, his obvious reaction was yet more lawfare. Sending me this latest missive headed "URGENT" in red is yet another example of Commercide's intimidatory tactics. I would rather go to jail than pay them a penny! So, on 25th April 2025 I sent Nick the following text message: "FUCK YOU"

Commercide Ventures are loan shark Mafioso in sharp suits and it's them who should be behind bars for all the crimes they have committed against us. So I will continue to write this book and speak out. How can my life be further destroyed apart from ceasing to be alive?

CAPITAL PUNISHMENT

When I look back on all the other stressful situations I've been through, I've realised they happen for you, not to you. For example, with "Dragons' Den" I learned so many lessons I had to write it all down to make sense of it all. If anyone had told me a few years prior that I'd be a published author I'd have said they were crazy.

I went on to do the after dinner speaking, which is the happiest I have ever been. The feeling you get when you're speaking in front of an audience and inspiring them is euphoric. To me, it's the best natural drug you can imagine!

Because I have to get my story out to the biggest audience possible, my TikTok platform has become my salvation. My purpose has been to grow it as big as I can to reach even more people. Being recognised for my "Dragons' Den" pitch pulled in a few thousand followers, but I could see that I could generate more interest if John and I shared our business knowledge for free.

Of course, the trolls soon started criticising our efforts. Our home address was made public within the first few days of being online. I believe it was someone with knowledge of Buildadeck's legal action against us, but I didn't waste my energy reporting them to the police because I knew it would be pointless.

For almost two years I've felt like a victim. But in the last two months my recovery has become my focus. I need to have my wits about me because my trust in people has gone. I now question who is my enemy, who is a real friend and who's on the fence. People have shown me their hands in different ways.

I haven't taken any of their behaviour personally. It has been too much for them to comprehend and they have their own issues to deal with. I don't blame them for avoiding us. Some people were scared and some thought I was crazy. I'd get silence and a confused look when I explained that if this could happen to us it could happen to them. It made them feel uncomfortable, so they avoided us. I am okay with being called crazy.

I notice so many broken people now. It's like I am now wearing a special pair of glasses. Our mental health has been affected since the lockdowns in 2020 and we are being squeezed so tightly with pressure in this scary world. I think corruption is at its worst right now and the uber rich cabal has misled and exploited every one of us.

A new breed of parasitic bankers and other elites have rigged the game for their own benefit. The rich now have massive political influence and are not only indifferent to anyone outside their economic bubble, they also want to ensure the divide is widened so far that they are untouchable. They literally want the world for themselves.

If all the private equity companies all do what Commercide did to me, they would have the monopoly on every service and need we require. They would find ways to confiscate our property due to the non-payment of a tax related to climate change or some other creative excuse.

I need to recover at speed so I can fight against this gradual push towards a dystopian future like so many others are doing now. Starting with me. I am trying to be the best version of myself. I am not chasing money or forcing relationships that are not meant to be. I have also looked at all my faults and corrected myself.

CAPITAL PUNISHMENT

I take accountability for my greed, for being manipulative, for not being the best mother, for not setting boundaries, for being impatient and at times being offensive. I will never go back to the person I once was. It's time for the new me.

I've had some horrible days these past two years, to the point where one evening I drove to the Humber Bridge and seriously considered throwing myself down into the freezing water. I felt so bad about making the decision that me and John were over. I remember bawling my eyes out, then switching on the radio and hearing the song "Going to the River to Pray." I said a prayer and I drove home. All emotions – even the most powerful – pass.

This world has become a frightening place, but a lot of it we have all brought on ourselves. It's the lack of understanding of ourselves and the lack of accountability for our actions that affect the future generations that are the main problems.

Tomorrow's world isn't built by governments or the elites. It's built by people like me who won't play by their rules. I never asked to be a fighter. Nobody has handed me anything for free. Tenacity is my superpower and if required, I will battle against tyranny and to expose lies until my last breath. I refuse to accept injustice and I feel like I have been tested since the moment I was born, because the adversity has been relentless.

I have been threatened by Commercide not to speak out about what they have done or write this book or they will take further legal action. At this point their threats are meaningless. They have already destroyed my life.

CAPITAL PUNISHMENT

I have spent the past few years in a state of constant fear with cortisol overloading my nervous system as I've tried to deal with all the lies, betrayals and family problems that have been swirling around in my head. All the sleepless nights and silent protests at the injustice of it all have put decades on my face.

In addition, all that time being so depressed and spending most of the time in my bedroom with the curtains closed getting very little sunlight or exercise has probably made me the perfect candidate for cancer. The body keeps the score they say. I am amazed that I still wake up every morning!

My marriage is now over and due to my suicide attempts I've lost my daughter's trust and can no longer see my granddaughters. I have no future and will probably never work again. I may as well be buried in the ground.

There is nothing more they can take from me.

Nick once told us, "Don't think you can take the suicidal way out of this." He knows he said this to put the idea in our heads. So my words right back at him are, "Don't think you can take closing down the company as your way out of this. I will make sure you never screw over another business ever again."

In April 2025 Buildadeck's lawyers and Commercide Ventures notified me that further punitive legal action will be taken if I talk or write about what they have done or post any more videos about it on social media.

My message to them remains the same. I refuse to be terrorised into compliance. I will continue to speak out about all the "legalised" crimes they have committed against myself and John.

CHAPTER 39

Another "Friend" Attempts to Silence Me

I was still receiving support from my mental health team and was so grateful for them agreeing that I shouldn't need to wait 18 months for trauma counselling. They'd seen my evidence and had validated that I was not imagining things.

John and I were living day to day, trying to get by. I had used the option with the bank to take a mortgage break. We were spending 24 hours a day together, but not by choice. Most of the time this past year I'd stayed in the bedroom and tried to sleep, while John sat at his computer preparing us for court. We were still tied to our newly built house because we had no spare funds to pay for separate accommodation.

I decided to go to my dad's house because I'd been getting around two hours' sleep. The first night in my childhood home made me feel comforted and safe, so now I was getting 7 hours at least, which is what you need to function. To relieve the boredom I was going to the gym, helping dad with the garden and catching up with friends when they were available.

One of them was called Neil. He'd upset me a little when I put my long YouTube video online, explaining what Commercide were doing to us and had asked me why I'd done it. I was a little surprised. He knew I needed the truth to be told, so why would he ask that question? His exact words had been, "I don't want to argue with you, but I don't agree with what you have done and you are asking for trouble."

It had been a few months since the video had been uploaded and we'd rekindled our friendship. He too was recovering from a mental breakdown because he hadn't dealt with the grief from the death of his mother as well as other issues. We swapped ideas on how to keep ourselves entertained now we were both sitting at home. I thought it would be a good idea to go for a walk in nature and he suggested we head out to Aysgarth Falls in the Yorkshire Dales.

I picked him up and drove the two-hour journey. Almost as soon as we set off Neil started lecturing me on how I should stop with the TikToks and that if Commercide's offer in court was to just drop hands and walk away, I should take it. He also said I should start a new business, get a new focus and put all this drama behind me.

I was stunned. Was he really suggesting that I should take the easy way, i.e., the coward's way out of this? Part of me understood why he was saying all this because I'd recently had that intimidating breach of settlement letter from Commercide's lawyers. After I opened it I fell apart and sobbed for days, distressed that they were trying to use fear as a weapon against me. It was the same feeling of shock I'd felt on the day we were served with the freezing order.

Neil suggested we pull over at the service station for a coffee and positioned himself opposite me at the table. Now it felt like an interrogation. His opinions on what I should do intensified. Irritated by his single-minded focus on my situation I asked if all this had happened to him would he just let it all go?

"Yes. They have more money than you. Plus, you don't have freedom of speech anymore. Most people would have stopped a long time ago," he replied.

"I'm not most people. Everyone that is putting me through this is well aware that I've been through it before with James Caan. I allowed myself to be persuaded to drop my lawsuit and hadn't fought my corner and that's not going to happen again."

This time all the lies, coercion and threats had hurt my soul. I even questioned my purpose on this earth. In the past I had so much courage. I'd achieved so much and that wasn't because I lived in fear. It's because I had strength and self-belief and that's all I needed to succeed.

"I can't live without accountability. I have to get justice this time," I explained.

I have watched this world the last five years with people being divided, people living in fear and authorities dictating rules on freedom of speech. I had even noticed everyone was too scared to even comment on my posts.

Every time I attempted to speak, Neil rolled his eyes and huffed. I was mortified. I felt like a naughty child being told off by their parent. Neil said he was nervous about the conversation he knew he needed to have with me and didn't want to argue. Up until now we've never had one cross word, so now I was confused. Why was he taking such an oppositional stance?

We got in the car and continued on to our destination, but it was obvious I was upset because I went very quiet. This was going to be a long, awkward drive. We parked the car at a café near the waterfalls. I was still mulling over Neil's comments, so I didn't take too much notice of the peaceful surroundings. Walking along the sides of the river with the cascading water and people milling about all I could think about was our recent conversation.

I took a couple of pictures of the river, but none of myself or Neil. I was dressed in a hoodie and wearing no makeup because I had nobody to impress. To my annoyance I noticed Neil was taking a video of me. I told him to stop. He didn't listen because after our walk he later sent me several videos and photos.

We walked back up the hill and stopped at a cafe for a coffee and cake. I was suddenly struck with a sense of déjà vu. Many years ago, Kevin Green from "The Secret Millionaire" had invited me to one of his talks. He was trying to persuade me to do after dinner speaking and invited me to a Nando's (because in his eyes that was all I was worth ha-ha!) to talk about it.

Soon after I arrived, he launched into his speech, warning me that I should give up my legal fight with James Caan and stop writing my book about "Dragons' Den." He said it would do more harm than good and I really didn't want to fall out with James. It was supposed to sound like good advice with a hint of a threat thrown in.

I had already done my research on Kevin Green and seen photos of him and James together when they were both in the running to be the new "dragon" on show. I knew James had sent him to get me to back off. This situation with Neil reminded me of that encounter so now I was wary, wondering who had made him try and influence me.

CAPITAL PUNISHMENT

Neil brought up the subject again of leaving everything alone to test if any of it was registering with me. For a split second he looked angry and frustrated. Was he on a mission and had to succeed or he wouldn't get paid? The thought crossed my mind, but I didn't dwell on it because there was no point. Neil would never tell me who was behind his efforts to change my mind.

As we walked back to the car we passed a large church. I hadn't even noticed it on our way down the hill. It was beautiful. I took off my hiking boots and put my trainers on, ready for the journey home. Then Neil said, "Why don't we have a look around the grounds of the church?"

As we made our way to the church, he pointed out the ages on the headstones and said, "That will be us if we don't have a purpose." Then he asked me if I'd consider going back into business and working with him. He said he regretted leaving his job after he'd had his breakdown and needed a purpose too.

I'd once told him I'd consider a business of some sort but not in the same industry as before. Putting this book together and promoting mental health awareness were my real passions. I'd learnt so much from inspirational people like Mel Robbins and other life coaches. (In fact I am writing another book after this one featuring all the healers who have helped me including the singer songwriter who produced my song. To just mention their names would not do them justice, so I am dedicating sections of my next book to every one of them. (They know who they are.)

As we walked back to the car we passed the church door. I checked to see if it was open and to my surprise it was. Neil held the door open for me, then he stepped inside the doorway and ventured no further.

"Aren't you coming in to say a prayer?" I asked.

He shook his head. My mind was racing.

"Don't you believe in God?"

He gave a slight nod but never spoke a word. The inside of the church was more like a cathedral. I knelt down at the altar, said a prayer and then turned to walk back. Neil was just putting his phone back in his pocket, so I don't know if he took another picture. If he did, he never sent it to me.

I was thinking about all the photos he'd taken after I'd asked him not to. It was the same as Freemason Paul. He'd made a TikTok video to show that he was at the Scunthorpe Museum. It looked like he was proving he'd seen me and had something on record. I couldn't help thinking Neil was doing the same thing.

The atmosphere was tense on the drive home. Now I'd be stuck next to him for two hours with no way to escape. I started panicking and was close to tears. Neil kept on repeating what I should do while I just listened. Now he was pissing me off. Eventually I burst into tears. Neil sat and watched me cry most of the way home. I don't remember if I asked him to stop talking, but I put the radio on so I didn't have to listen to him anymore. When we reached his house he made one last attempt to talk his version of sense into me.

"Listen Neil," I said angrily, "I don't expect you to understand what this company has done to me. You'll never experience the pain and anguish I have. You have no right to tell me what to do."

I drove off and when I reached the motorway I pulled in a layby and sobbed like I've never sobbed before. It was though everyone thought I was deluded and my tenacity and stubbornness were my worst enemies. Five hours later, when I'd cried my tears dry I arrived home and crawled into bed, falling straight asleep from exhaustion.

I spent the next day in a trance. My mood was really low and I felt irritated. I did my dad's shopping early the next morning and told him I'd be busy for the day. I didn't want him to see how depressed I was. So I went back to my house in the country, sat down and just gazed out of the window at the river and the birds flying by.

I sent a text to my counsellor Trish to tell her I wouldn't be starting therapy with Jenny the following week. It would be a waste of public money that would be better spent on someone who actually had a future. Then I contacted the court to see how long it would be before the judge gave us a response to our application for a strike out. Every time I called the line was busy. I was so miserable I could barely breathe. It was scary how quickly I'd fallen.

Only a few days earlier I'd heard an ice cream van somewhere nearby and asked my dad if he wanted an ice cream. While I sat on the wall and waited, I chatted to a woman with a child of around the age of 7 until the van came around the corner. I asked the girl if she wanted an ice cream. She looked up at her mum and said, "Can I?" Her mum agreed. The look on that little girl's face gave me the most amazing feeling.

CAPITAL PUNISHMENT

As my dad and I sat eating our Mr Whippy 99s on the back patio I thought, "I feel happy and content." The weights on my shoulders had been temporarily lifted by that one good deed.

Trish called and asked if she could come and see me. I told her that I was deluded and my book was never going to reach anybody. The posts to my social media platforms were being shadow banned because views had dwindled to a couple of hundred whereas before they were in the thousands. My self-belief had gone as well as any hope I could publicise my story.

Jenny, my therapist called and I told her that everything felt pointless. I just wanted to release my book and leave this world for good. Trish came straight to my house with a colleague because she was really worried about me. I'd been this low a few times since starting my counselling a few weeks ago. This was pretty much all I had to pass my time, except for an hour at the gym and a bit of shopping for my dad. The rest of the time I had nothing to distract my mind and just ruminated on the lawsuit all day and night.

I remembered one doctor telling me there was a fine line between genius and insanity and many intelligent people are prone to emotional pain due to self-criticism and over-thinking. Doing nothing made me feel suffocated. My life felt soulless. I had no purpose, no sense of belonging and no long-term goals.

Trish suggested I do some voluntary work and said she knew someone who could arrange for me to work with the start-up businesses until I decided what my next move would be. I agreed, which proved there was still a tiny smidgen of hope for me.

I knew I could never move on until I knew the perpetrators of the crimes against me had been held accountable for what they had done. I was trapped in victimhood. It felt like I was stuck in treacle and could barely move.

Desperate to hear something encouraging, I popped my head around the bedroom door to say goodnight to my dad. I confessed to him everything that had happened the past few days. He told me I'd get through and that he believed in God and everything happens for a reason. I told him I loved him and turned in for the night.

A few hours later I woke up and realised why I had been so triggered. Yet again I'd allowed a "friend" to force their opinions onto me. Would a real friend seeing you in so much pain want to add more? I sent Neil a text:

"I have sat and thought about this before sending this message. I had to call my therapist today and they had to come and see me because after meeting you on Saturday I lost my power. I don't want to be horrible and I wish you all the best but I couldn't look for a business with you. You made me feel so shitty forcing your opinions on me and telling me what to do. Every time I tried to explain my side of things you rolled your eyes and dismissed my pain and trauma. I have to do what's right for me to get over what's happened."

Getting my book out there and making the criminals in my life accountable are what I need to move on. Surely friends support each other, like I did you. I never made you feel bad. I just think I need to be in business on my own because then I can be me and be responsible for myself. I want you to find your purpose too."

I closed my eyes and slept until late the next morning. When I woke up I had received another email from Commercide's lawyers.

My heart pounded while I searched for my glasses. I knew exactly what the email was going to say. Had they sent this so there was an excuse to keep my house under the freezing order? This time the fear passed through me and I didn't allow it to stay.

CHAPTER 40

"Unclean Hands"

On May 1st I received an email titled: "URGENT: NOTICE OF BREACH OF SETTLEMENT AGREEMENT" stating that Buildadeck is "actively considering the options available to it."

One of these is that they would be "relieved of any ongoing obligations to you under the Settlement Agreement" not to sue me to recover the money I was paid for the sale of my company to them and not demand the return of my three months' severance pay.

As I have stated many times, they know full well that when that agreement was signed, Nick and all the directors had agreed to allow me to make purchases via Buildadeck and offset them against my deferred interest. In reality I am still owed £300,000 plus the value of my 14% share in the company, while John is owed his 70%.

Interestingly, John ran the letter through ChatGPT and it came up with some very good points:

My posts, videos and messages, especially if emotional or reactive, should be viewed in the light of Buildadeck and Commercide's own conduct. This includes the non-disclosure of the Settlement Agreement at their December 15th hearing for their application for a freezing order and litigation designed to bankrupt me and take my home.

CAPITAL PUNISHMENT

Other factors to take into consideration are the emotional distress caused by freezing my only major asset (my house), while I have no income, no legal team and serious mental health challenges. Severe psychological pain and suffering that is intentionally inflicted by continually subjecting someone to unwarranted stress and punishment is known to cause permanent mental damage and can drive its victims to suicide.

My posts, even if critical or confrontational, were a natural emotional response to extreme legal pressure and not malicious defamation. They were acts of self defence, not attacks because I was trying to reclaim my narrative after being falsely accused of theft, sacked without process and threatened with ruin. By law you are allowed to provide information in your own defence and you are also allowed to retaliate against someone who has slandered or defamed you.

Even if I did breach the agreement by speaking out, the letter confirms the Settlement Agreement is now being used to suppress legitimate criticism. Despite knowing that I have no money, no lawyer, and mental health issues they are threatening to recover £37,500, sue for further damages and seek costs.

This action is not about justice; it's a coercive tactic to stop me from exposing misconduct. Their disproportionate reaction suggests the agreement is being used as a litigation trap.

My videos describe the threats relating to my home. The letter doesn't deny these; it only complains about me telling my story which supports the claim that their goal is to seize my property and not resolve a genuine dispute. Their pressure is punitive, not remedial which is a hallmark of abuse of process.

In conclusion, the letter from Commercide and Buildadeck shows the Settlement Agreement Is being weaponised and is proof of intimidation and retaliation. It also reveals that Commercide is actively behind the litigation and threats, even if they are not formally named as a claimant, which suggests collusion and a coordinated campaign of intimidation.

Commercide has demonstrated an abuse of process, which in legal terms means they have "unclean hands." They have acted unconscionably by seeking injunctions and claw backs while concealing the Settlement Agreement, not disclosing key facts at the injunction hearing and sending letters like this one designed to suppress free speech and silence whistleblowing. Any claim to recover my termination payment should be struck out on this basis.

Commercide are in breach of the agreement by putting their charges against you in the public domain. These charges refer to matters that were already known to them at the time of signing. The Settlement Agreement cannot be selectively applied to one party.

I thought this was an incredibly accurate assessment of Nick's legal team's latest attempts to silence me and break my spirit.

Commercide knows the foundations on which their claims against us are built on sand. So any subsequent injunctions will be equally groundless. The more legal weaponry they attack me with now, the worse they will look when all this comes out at trial and the bigger my damages claim against them will be, especially if their lies end up putting me in jail. For this reason, all their warnings and threats are self-incriminating and self-destructive at this point.

CAPITAL PUNISHMENT

What these predators do not realise is that when you've lost everything you have worked for, when all your boundaries have been crossed and your honesty has been exploited you have nothing left to lose. This is when you become most dangerous.

The worst-case scenario is that I may go to jail or lose my house. But now I just think, "Take it!" I will not be threatened with punishments and consequences for speaking out about the crimes that are being committed via corporate lawyers working on behalf of their greedy, ruthless overlords. I am already in a virtual jail cell, restricted as to what I can do, unable to live freely, sell my house or move on.

All I want now is for my voice to be heard and to be recognised and appreciated for who I truly am. I can't change what has happened in the past, but I do grieve all the time and opportunities I have now lost.

Nobody is coming to save me. Only I can save myself. I know all my haters and the predators at Commercide Ventures are willing me to give up and fail.

But I will show them that I will not only succeed, I will triumph.

Thanks to My Good Friends

I have always had a small handful of friends but in circumstances like these, they have fallen into one of three categories.

There are the ones who want to believe you but are scared to get involved. There are the ones that don't believe you and think you are crazy. Then there is the smallest group of all: the ones that believe you because they know you inside out - usually over many years - and want to help you.

While the events leading up to the experience of trauma are always unique to that person, the sheer feeling of despair when you reach that point is commonly shared.

Neil and I reached that point almost simultaneously. Although we had been friends for a long time our unique yet similar set of circumstances gave us a commonality words cannot explain. We became each other's crutch and ultimately helped to pull each other away from the edge of the abyss.

Many people, me included, assume that everyone wants the same thing: to be as successful as possible with tons of money in the bank. A lot of people have aspired to be like me saying things like, "It must be great being so rich. Aren't you lucky!"

If they only knew the inner torment, the trials and sacrifices business owners go through on an almost daily basis. Maybe it's them that are the lucky ones with all their free time and far less responsibilities and pressure. Another sad fact is that most people spend all their time working hard to make people like or even love them. The reality that if they simply liked even loved themselves others would too.

Another of my friends, John Leppington of Digital Cookie Media, while believing what I was going through, was concerned that in searching for the truth I could easily start seeing shadows in places where there was no light. In other words, adding two and two and getting five.

Fortunately, he did not abandon me and has been a rock from a distance, keeping me grounded and escorting me on this journey. At times this has been to his own detriment, so for that I will be eternally grateful. His video and graphic skills are also fantastic. So I would like to thank him for giving me courage to put my story out in the public domain so I can say I have done my part to warn others.

Since I was 17 there has been one friend who has always been there, never questioned or doubted me, never second guessed or undermined me. I know she will always be there for me, as I will for her. That is my BFF Christine.

At school I was part of a terrible trio: me, Dianne and Wendy. We could go years without speaking or seeing each other but we seemed to have inbuilt radars and knew when someone needed us. As Wendy lived in London there were limited times that we were all together. The last time we all met was the night my "Dragons' Den" episode was aired. It was as if we were still at school. Our weird sense of humour and friendship was the perfect balance that worked.

CAPITAL PUNISHMENT

Wendy had recently separated from her childhood sweetheart so now we were all in the same boat being single parents. My friends both knew how lonely I felt and had asked if I wanted to do something that day. They knew my heart was breaking for Molly and didn't want me to be on my own.

We planned to visit a well-known café called "The Pink Pig." It was a local landmark and a place Scunthorpe was proud of, being part of an organic, wholesome, family-run farm. I collected my friends and we started to reminisce.

We laughed about the local boys we fancied. Mine was Steve Proctor, Christine's was Gaz Macalenny and Wendy's was Chris Wooton. Wendy commented that she completely went off Steve when we saw him kick a hedgehog 30 feet into the air and killed it. All his mates thought it was amusing but we were horrified.

As we sat at the café table Martin Macalenny, Gaz's brother, was right behind us. How bizarre was that? We said, "We've just been talking about you!" We mentioned the horrible time Steve had kicked the hedgehog and Martin's face dropped. He said, "Have you not heard about Steve? He just lost his leg from sepsis from the hip down." We stared in silence with open mouths. Was that karma for killing the hedgehog?

I was saddened to hear this news and wished Steve a speedy recovery. He's really a lovely guy with an amazing wife Lisa. I hope with the support from his family he can turn this into something positive because he didn't deserve this.

Afterwards, as we walked through the park, Wendy asked if anyone had seen Kim Burnet? We'd spent a lot of our younger years with

Kim, a little "pocket rocket" who still was as beautiful in her early twenties. Just as I was telling my friends I'd had a text from her, a Mini pulled into the carpark. It was Kim! Omg!

That day could not have gone any better or made me feel so comforted. It felt like God was watching down on us the whole day. In times of need these friends have always had my back and I will love them forever.

Finally, there's my good friend and editor Karina. Although we are 1,500 miles apart and live in different time zones, she has been there for me every second I've needed her. While fighting her own personal battles she's never wavered in her support. If there are any grammatical errors in this book, blame her lol!

Thanks to My Family

Molly will always be my world but I have newfound respect for her taking control of her life and seeing what's true. Me and her dad Rob broke up when she was three years of age. Apart from the tensions from the initial separation we navigated our own paths independently and moved onto pastures new. Rob went on to build a new life and gave Molly two new siblings.

We agreed that Rob could see Molly whenever he wanted but it would usually be two nights a week. There was no animosity. I took accountability for the reasons we broke up in the first place. I suffered trauma from my childhood that was never mended which overflowed into the relationship.

Learning how to control your emotions and your reactions isn't something you can go to the supermarket and purchase then come home to reprogramme your brain. It's a skill you learn at a very early age and is passed down the generations. I can only pass on what I learned too and will never be able to apologise enough to Molly for my failings.

Everyone sets out in life striving to make the best in choices and decisions. It's only when you have a deep understanding of life in general and the paths, we choose that you can stand up and take accountability and recover from past trauma. Before that, I accepted the help on offer but it was just a plaster to cover the hurt.

Molly witnessed situations and decisions where I thought I was doing the best for us both. It's only now that I truly appreciate how this affected her too. She has always accepted me and has watched my life unfold in front of her eyes. She looked up to me and I got it wrong.

After the shock events of December 2023 and my suicide attempt Molly withdrew from me emotionally. I felt it and so did she. My time with her children was now supervised because she felt she had to protect her precious cargo. I broke her trust and shocked her deeply when I tried to end my life.

She witnessed a further 14 months of me struggling while I eventually figured things out. Sadly, because we were both extremely defensive and scared there were many hurtful actions and words that were spoken on both sides.

There comes a time in everyone's life when they need to take a long hard look in the mirror. Some people are fortunate enough to like what they see while others will see the errors they have made and the people they have hurt.

I was forced to look at myself and admit that I did not like what I saw. I feel I have at times been selfish, manipulative and controlling. But on a positive note, I also saw the love I am capable of giving. I can't fail to show empathy towards others even though they may have wronged me. It has been a humbled process of self-discovery.

Hopefully if she ever looks, she will see what I see: her beauty and intelligence and the caring giving woman and mother she has grown to be. Molly, I love you with all my heart.

Of course, I must thank my husband John for loving me for the person I am. John and I have sat in pain in our own heads day and night for so long we cannot help but look at our actions from the past and think about all the "if onlys" and what we could have done to prevent the ordeals we have been through. I wish him well on the next part of his life's journey and will always be here when he needs me.

CAPITAL PUNISHMENT

Final Thoughts

Anyone who knows me and John would know that we have grafted all our lives, working ridiculous hours seven days a week. This has caused us both to neglect the simple things in life we should have experienced and lost us time that should have been spent with our loved ones.

It's very sad, because if we had died our eulogies would have been all about how we worked so hard and ended up with nothing. What a waste of our lives! It's ironic because we strived so hard to be successful to make us feel like we weren't worthless. We thought making money was the only thing we were good at that made other people happy. This is because we had to earn our love as children. Both of us only received love when it was given as a reward, which is the case with so many entrepreneurs.

My control issues are a way of avoiding the pain of things going wrong and to stop the same mistake being repeated. I tried to make others adopt my controlling ways, not out of malice, but so they too could avoid painful mistakes. But I realise now that life is about learning your own lessons, because that's what makes us grow.

My lack of patience was me not getting my own way. I demanded the same ethos in others that I demanded of myself. If I say I will do it right there and then. If I am at fault, I will quickly put things right to avoid upsetting others.

But not everyone has the same ethos as me. I'd treat people kindly until they let me down and I'd respond with frustration and anger.

CAPITAL PUNISHMENT

Now I see that I can only be responsible for my own actions, not those of others and should not punish people for not thinking the way I do.

I see this life in this world today as being similar to "The Hunger Games" rather than the perfect world I have always strived to create. If I can help someone I will. If I can prevent someone from suffering I will. That's because I have suffered during my whole life and became a people pleaser and failed to set boundaries to prevent other people abusing me.

The most amazing emotions I've ever felt in my life have always been when I'm helping others, whether financially or any other way. Usually it's only for an hour or so, but it's an intense feeling of pride and satisfaction. Sadly, people tend to forget all the kind things you have done for them along the way. If everyone could help each other, and share the love, we could all have those feelings. This is where I believe the world could change and start a ripple effect.

I buy homeless people bags full of food. (I've never given money because quite often they have addictions) but that moment of appreciation makes me feel good even if it's just for a few short minutes. I've bought flowers in a shop and when the shop keeper has taken the payment, I've handed them right back and said, "These are for you."

I have stood in queues with small children in front of me hearing their struggling mother explaining they didn't have the money to buy treats and toys. Then I'd buy the children whatever it was they wanted, chase after them and ask if it was okay for me to give it to them. I have been thanked by many grateful mothers.

My best friend works long hours and is a single parent. I watched her getting stressed because she couldn't afford to buy her daughter a car and saw her anguish when she was seeing what she could sell. So I went out and bought a car for her and paid the first year of the insurance. Being kind is the best feeling there is.

John and I spent three days together checking through every piece of evidence we have mentioned in the book. During this time, we left all the anger and disappointment behind us. It was a pleasure to be with him again. We both realised even though we'd only spent seven weeks apart, it had given us time to reflect on our journey.

Things that annoyed me before were still there, but I didn't have the same level of irritation as I had before. If I asked John a question that required a very simple answer of yes or no, one of my irritations was he would ask another 15 questions before he gave an answer. It was a bugbear of mine, but now we could laugh about it.

We also discussed the lessons we had learned along the way. John admitted he had always chased money. I had told him so many times in the past, never chase money, chase success and the money will naturally come. He had time to reflect on this comment and saw I was right.

We talked about our relationship and he questioned if anything could be rekindled. I had to be honest; I did still love and care for him, but even after the intense fear of what's ahead of us had gone, my feelings hadn't changed.

I believe we are twin flames and we were meant to come together for a reason. He had experience with Mitu Misra and I had mine with James Caan, then we both suffered this nightmare with the

CAPITAL PUNISHMENT

Americans. Unfortunately, when something has been broken, you can't just cover over the pieces with sticky tape.

I told him we would always be in each other's lives and he felt the same, but our season had passed and it is time for both of us to move on.

The sadness is still there because ending any relationship, especially when you are married, is very hard emotionally. John will always be my special person. Nobody will ever understand what we have both been through except us. I think I have cried every single day for the last year without fail.

In the past we allowed fear and control to crush the small amount of self-esteem we both had. Now we have both had the chance to build on that lesson and do things differently. I have faced my shadows through talking to counsellors and now clearly see that John has been on his own journey too. It's time for him to take the rest of his life in the direction he chooses now just as I plan to do. He's a survivor and I know he will be fine as will I.

At the beginning of May 2025, I had received a second warning letter from the American's solicitors, giving me six days to respond. They were demanding that I gave them assurance that I will not dispose of the TikTok videos or Facebook posts I have made, presumably for legal purposes. They also wanted assurance that I

would not talk about their company or its CEO or mention him in this book.

When I received their first warning, they had seen the YouTube and TikTok videos I had posted titled "The Little Rat" where I had described the atrocious allegations against me and named the CEO. I removed and deleted them both, even though it pained me to do so.

Their second letter was hand delivered as well as served by email and was written in a far much more serious and threatening tone. John and I had been so busy fact checking the book we hadn't given it a second thought. But now the book was finished and almost ready to upload to Amazon, I remembered I needed to respond.

We discussed the best and worst scenarios that could happen. John looked at me and said, "I can accept things easier than you and what will be will be," meaning he could let everything go and put it behind him and not publish our account of the facts.

I explained to him that I can do that in many situations, but not when it comes to matters of my integrity. We have stolen nothing. It was them who stole from us. Like I've said before, I hate liars and these bully boys can't get away with what they have done.

I gave all my haters the chance to apologise and that's all I've ever asked for, an apology I recently uploaded a TikTok video saying these very words. I don't know if any of our accusers saw it, but there was no response from them. Instead of looking at the immorality of their actions they have doubled down on their vicious lawfare campaign.

John then admitted maybe this was another lesson he needed to learn. He had rolled over far too quickly with Mitu and should have appealed his case. So, this time he said he would support me.

He knows I'll never be able to move on unless Commercide takes accountability for the inhumane level of mental torture we have been subjected to as a result of their false and unsubstantiated claims. This is why he is prepared to back me, gamble the house and let fate lead the way.

Epilogue

On May 9th 2025 I received the most wonderful email from one of our colleagues at Buildadeck. It was so unexpected and so incredibly important it made me cry. Here is a copy of the statement that changes everything for John and I:

WITNESS STATEMENT
Re: John Ross and Sharon Wright

"I first met John Ross and Dan Jones on 4th July 2020 when I was interviewed for the role of Design Consultant for Buildadeck Decking. When I started, Buildadeck's turnover was in the region of £5 million per year.

During my interview John Ross shared his ambition to build a UK network of Design Consultants and make Buildadeck the largest UK company selling direct to UK consumers. It was evident that John had the experience, talent and desire to deliver on his ambition. He was a real leader and it was a pleasure to be part of a team that was led by such a dynamic and ambitious individual.

During my time at Buildadeck I delivered circa £1.5 million per year and under John's leadership and guidance, I was promoted to Sales Manager and helped recruit and train a network of UK Design consultants delivering up to £6 million per year in domestic sales. Under John's leadership Buildadeck's revenue grew to around £25 million per year.

CAPITAL PUNISHMENT

During my time at Buildadeck I was aware that John Ross and Sharon Wright were the driving forces behind the growth with Sharon concentrating on the expanding commercial business with holiday parks.

On occasion, Dan would speak to me about Sharon. He was always derogatory, claiming John was his friend and Sharon was a nightmare. He described her as a person that was not beneficial to the business and that he wished she was not part of Buildadeck at all. He used derogatory adjectives on the few occasions we discussed SW and his perception of her.

I did not know Sharon personally, however I engaged with her on a number of occasions through referrals she brought to the domestic business. We conducted phone closes together on around £100,000 of domestic sales. These were all introductions from Sharon from her network. My experience has always been a positive and uplifting one whenever I worked with her.

In April 2023 Dan told me that John and Sharon had left the business. He told me they had decided to sell their shares to the investors and leave the business. It was all very sudden and none of it made sense.

I immediately contacted John by text to congratulate him on his retirement as I knew that the story being used wasn't true. I also stated that if he were to ever come out of retirement I would leave Buildadeck join him, as I knew the management team running Buildadeck weren't qualified to do so and that John and Sharon leaving would be to the detriment of the business and ultimately my livelihood.

Eventually Dan confided in me that the situation with John and Sharon was serious and that they had fraudulently used Buildadeck to finance their new house build and they (Buildadeck) were going to issue criminal proceedings.

I thought this was strange as I know that Dan had arranged for a number of suppliers to meet him on site with regard to the house build. On numerous occasions he would be on site meeting suppliers for Johns new house build. I know this as I phoned Dan daily to update him on sales and he would tell me where was.

In the last few months of my time at Buildadeck I was seconded to look after commercial holiday parks in Yorkshire and the East Coast as a large number of sales staff had left. A large number of people left Buildadeck between April 2023 and December 2024). Sales were down significantly and the feedback from Dan was that the business was losing significant money.

In the time I worked within the commercial sector of Holiday Parks I met a number of park owners that asked about Sharon. Many of them were new accounts that she had won a number of years ago. The park owners remembered her fondly and commented that she worked incredibly hard, long hours and in all weathers and nothing would be too much trouble. They asked me to pass on their best wishes to her which I did by text.

There were two owners that were very dissatisfied with the level of customer service that they were now experiencing due to Buildadeck's inability to address quality issues and do remedial work. They commented that whenever there was a problem Sharon would sort it out immediately. They had not experienced a high level of service since Sharon left.

This statement is the first time I have commented on John Ross or Sharon Wright. The treatment by Buildadeck and their campaign to discredit them is disgusting."

This statement is important for several reasons. It clearly proves that everyone in the management team knew about the building material purchases being offset against my deferred consideration. It supports the fact that John and I are not thieves and did not steal from the company on the sly and the allegations against us are false.

It also proves that Paul has lied in his statement and Nick and Commercide have conspired to devise a vile plot to defraud us of our shares, renege on their agreement to fully pay me for my company and get their hands on my house.

Dan was once John's long-time friend and worked with him before Buildadeck. He replaced me as Buildadeck's sales director, although in my opinion he did not have the ability, personality or drive for the job. Another reason he didn't like me was because I once said he was arrogant and chauvinistic, plus I didn't trust him. If I challenged him on anything he never looked me in the eye. I tried to give him the benefit of the doubt because John didn't have many friends and he'd known this guy for decades.

After John and I were fired and before we were served with the lawsuit, we all went out together and Dan got extremely drunk back at our house. He turned on me and said, "All this shit with Buildadeck is your fault. You were too soft and let the customers walk over you. Your install times and repairs were totally unrealistic. You should offer Commercide £200 grand out of what they've paid you because it isn't possible to run the install companies the way you did."

I was mortified and burst into tears. Dan realised he'd said too much and went quiet while John furiously defended me saying, "It was because of Sharon we did so well! "She doesn't owe them anything either!"

Too upset to be in Dan's company I went upstairs. Then I heard shouting and quickly ran back downstairs. They'd both been drinking and I was scared things would turn violent. I got there just in time to see John literally kicking Dan out of the house.

The next day I was so confused. Why had he said I should offer Commercide £200,000? A few days later, I encourage John to patch thing up with Dan and their friendship continued until Dan let him down about going into business with him and accepted a payoff from Commercide for not going ahead with the idea.

Now it all made sense. It was Dan who'd told Declan Amble to delay our payment from the insurance company. The builder said one of Buildadeck's directors who lived in Leeds had mentioned the idea. That could only be Dan. He was the snake in the grass who had plotted against us with Commercide.

CAPITAL PUNISHMENT

John has since spoken to the author of this statement and he says several other members of the management team are also prepared to come forward and stand up as witnesses in court to speak in our defence.

Get ready for Capital Punishment 2!

Thank you for Reading this Book

I really appreciate that you have taken the time to find out more about the situation John and I are in. We would appreciate any support we can get. If you can help us in our fight we would love to hear from you.

To contact me please send an email to **sharon@sharonwright.com**

To find out more about my appearance on "Dragons' Den" please visit: **wwwsharonwrightdragonslayer.com**

Printed in Great Britain
by Amazon